SpringerBriefs in Economics

Kobe University Social Science Research Series

The Kobe University Social Science Research Series has been established as a subseries of the SpringerBrief in Economics Series, but in fact this exciting interdisciplinary collection encompasses scholarly research not only in the economics but also in law, political science, business and management, accounting, international relations, and other subdisciplines within the social sciences. As a national university with a special strength in the social sciences, Kobe University actively promotes interdisciplinary research. This series is not limited only to research emerging from Kobe University's faculties of social sciences but also welcomes cross-disciplinary research that integrates studies in the arts and sciences.

Kobe University, founded in 1902, is the second oldest national higher education institution for commerce in Japan and is now a preeminent institution for social science research and education in the country. Currently, the social sciences section includes four faculties — Law, Economics, Business Administration, and International Cooperation Studies — and the Research Institute for Economics and Business Administration (RIEB). There are some 230-plus researchers who belong to these faculties and conduct joint research through the Center for Social Systems Innovation and the Organization for Advanced and Integrated Research, Kobe University. This book series comprises academic works by researchers in the social sciences at Kobe University as well as their collaborators at affiliated institutions, Kobe University alumni and their colleagues, and renowned scholars from around the world who have worked with academic staff at Kobe University. Although traditionally the research of Japanese scholars has been publicized mainly in the Japanese language, Kobe University strives to promote publication and dissemination of works in English in order to further contribute to the global academic community.

Horst Hanusch • Yasushi Hara

Innovative Growth and Climate Security

The Quest for Global Transformation

Springer

Horst Hanusch
Faculty of Business and Economics
University of Augsburg
Bad Wiessee, Bayern, Germany

Yasushi Hara
Faculty of Business Administration
Kobe University
Kobe, Japan

ISSN 2191-5504 ISSN 2191-5512 (electronic)
SpringerBriefs in Economics
ISSN 2520-1697 ISSN 2520-1700 (electronic)
Kobe University Social Science Research Series
ISBN 978-981-92-1004-6 ISBN 978-981-92-1005-3 (eBook)
https://doi.org/10.1007/978-981-92-1005-3

This Springer imprint is published by the registered company Springer Nature Singapore Pte Ltd.
The registered company address is: 152 Beach Road, #21-01/04 Gateway East, Singapore 189721, Singapore

Preface

The global economy stands at a critical juncture, marked by a profound paradox. On the one hand, the Schumpeterian engine of innovation, driven by emerging technologies such as artificial intelligence and digitalisation, promises unprecedented progress and prosperity. On the other hand, the escalating climate crisis, anticipated by thinkers such as Georgescu-Roegen, threatens the ecological foundations of human existence. We appear to be advancing simultaneously towards a potential 'Garden of Eden' and on the brink of ecological collapse. How can these powerful yet seemingly contradictory forces be reconciled? How might societies sustain innovation and economic growth while ensuring long-term security on a finite planet?

This book arises from the conviction that existing economic frameworks are inadequate for understanding, let alone addressing, this foundational challenge. Although traditional models of economic development were successful in the twentieth century, they failed to incorporate the 'social costs' of environmental degradation effectively. This work seeks to address that gap by proposing a new analytical approach: Post-Schumpeterian Economics (PSE). The aim is to extend Joseph Schumpeter's insights into innovation, creative destruction, and economic evolution to meet the challenges of the twenty-first century, marked by global existential risks. PSE offers a synthesis of economic dynamism and ecological responsibility, advancing a hybrid conception of sustainable development.

The book is organised into two chapters. Chapter 2 establishes the theoretical foundations of this approach, tracing the intellectual trajectory from classical Schumpeterian thought through Neo-Schumpeterian economics to the ecologically attuned framework of PSE. It explores strategic levers for global transformation, including market-based mechanisms and state-led technology policies.

Chapter 3 shifts from theory to empirical analysis. Drawing on a comprehensive dataset and employing extensive cluster analysis, it examines the ongoing transformation across the G-20 nations. The result is a data-driven typology of diverse transition pathways pursued by major economies. Comparative analyses of the G-7 and BRICS blocs reveal a heterogeneous landscape. Rather than a singular 'Quest for Global Transformation', multiple archetypes emerge: from the innovation-led, high-risk approaches of the United States and China, to the more balanced, policy-driven strategies in Europe, and the diverse trajectories evident among large emerging economies.

This book is intended for scholars, students, and policymakers in economics, innovation studies, environmental policy, and international relations. We hope that the Post-Schumpeterian framework and the empirical findings presented herein will offer a novel and useful perspective on one of the most urgent and complex challenges of our time.

Bad Wiessee, Bayern, Germany
Kobe, Japan
September 2025

Horst Hanusch
Yasushi Hara

Acknowledgements

A project of this scale is never the product of the authors' efforts alone. We would like to express our sincere gratitude to the friends, colleagues, and family members who have supported us throughout the long process of writing this book.

Our academic journey has been greatly enriched by discussions with our colleagues. We extend our heartfelt thanks to Professor Andreas Pyka of the University of Hohenheim and Professor Uwe Cantner of the Friedrich-Schiller-Universität Jena for their insightful comments, stimulating debates, and unwavering encouragement. Their expertise in the field of innovation economics has been an invaluable source of inspiration and has significantly shaped the arguments presented in these pages. Earlier versions of this work were also presented at several academic gatherings, and we are grateful for the valuable feedback we received from the participants of the 19th East Asian Economic Association International Conference, the Asia Pacific Innovation Conference 2024, and the International Schumpeter Society Conference 2024. These discussions helped us to refine and sharpen our arguments.

This book would not have been possible without the patience, understanding, and steadfast support of our families. We are deeply grateful to Maria Hanusch, Konstanze Hanusch, and Yuka Kudo-Hara for their enduring encouragement and for providing the foundation of support that allowed us to dedicate our time and energy to this research.

While we have benefited immensely from the support of many, any errors or omissions that remain are, of course, our own.

Contents

About the Authors

Horst Hanusch Professor emeritus, Institute of Economics, University of Augsburg. During his academic career, he wrote and published numerous books and articles on Public Economics and Schumpeterian Theory. He is the co-founder (together with Wolfgang Stolper) of the International Joseph A. Schumpeter Society and was its Secretary General until 2022. He is also the Founding Editor of the *Journal of Evolutionary Economics* and Honorary President of the International Institute of Public Finance. His current research interests focus on a Post-Schumpeterian framework for Public Finance as well as Economic Development Theory.

Yasushi Hara Associate Professor, Graduate School of Business Administration, Kobe University. Prior to his current position, which he has held since April 2022, he served as a research associate at the Institute of Innovation Research, Hitotsubashi University; a researcher at the Science, Technology and Innovation Policy Research Center (SciREX Center) at the National Graduate Institute for Policy Studies (GRIPS); a Michelin Fellow at the France-Japan Research Center on Contemporary Japan (CEAFJP/EHESS) at the School of Advanced Studies in the Social Sciences in Paris; and a lecturer at the Graduate School of Economics, Hitotsubashi University, Tokyo, Japan.

Chapter 1
Introduction

"Big History", a new scientific discipline, has recently produced two remarkable publications: first, the internationally highly successful book by Yuval Noah Harari, entitled "Homo Deus" (2017), and second, a treatise by David Christians entitled "Big History: Between Nothing and Everything" (Christian et al., 2013), which arguably gave its name to the entire field of science. Both books excellently characterize the ambivalent situation we find ourselves in today when thinking about the future development of our planet. Harari, on the one hand, promises the birth of a new technological age, in which creative human beings and intelligent machines together will form a wonderful symbiosis, producing a "Garden of Eden", with an incredible potential of fruitful effects for the progress and prosperity of mankind.

Christian's book, on the other hand, tells a diametrically opposed story of human development. Analytically outstanding, he focuses on the fundamental negative effects that the anthropocene economy has produced since the Technological Revolution more than 200 years ago, namely climate change that threatens the very existence of the planet and an exponentially growing loss of biodiversity.

As an economist, one does not actually have to resort to the findings of "Big History" if one wants to emphasize the elementary ambivalence of the two development scenarios. A dogma-historical look at one's own discipline is sufficient.

In the years 1934 to 1936 two genius economists worked closely together at Harvard University, Joseph A. Schumpeter and N. Georgescu-Roegen. This was the time when Schumpeter's magnus opus "Die Theorie der wirtschaftlichen Entwicklung" had already been published in the 4th edition and when his interest concentrated on supplementing the "Theory" with statistical and historical material. For Georgescu-Roegen this period has to be considered more or less "an apprenticeship". His main contributions to economic science were published much later with the beginning of the 50s when Schumpeter was already dead. But he was always proud of having been a pupil of Schumpeter and he often stressed the immense influence which Schumpeterian ideas had on the development of his own intellectual career.

H. Hanusch, Y. Hara, *Innovative Growth and Climate Security*, SpringerBriefs in Economics, https://doi.org/10.1007/978-981-92-1005-3_1

Comparing both economists isn't an easy task, but it gives an enormous insight into how capitalism is working since the industrial revolution and which results concerning future growth and development highly technologized economies may expect.

Schumpeter is regarded as one of the most important economists of the twentieth century. He is a "giant" visionary who is able to elucidate capitalism's economic vigor ingeniously, portraying it as a force propelling towards an open future and deriving creative impetus from innovative changes, both micro and macro. This dynamism spawns economic development, evidenced historically in eminent growth rates of GNP, in the Western Hemisphere during the last 200 years, in Asia after World War II. For him capitalism is the most promising form to organize an economy. Nowadays, such ideas influence remarkably the strategy and philosophy of modern capitalism in its varieties of realization: In a more entrepreneurial and liberal form shaping business in the US Silicon Valley. Or, in a more collective or autocratic design as a system of "state or command capitalism" prevalent in the People's Republic of China.

Fundamentally linked to this huge quantitative economic success in the Western hemisphere transitions of a societal nature were underway, changing the living conditions of individual households and firms, as history can also prove. Starting with the technological revolution in Great Britain at the end of the eighteenth century, the socio-economic interplay of economic agents in the West of our planet developed in the nineteenth and twentieth centuries, mostly technologically determined, from pre-industrial to industrial societies and, especially in the USA, to a post-industrial socioeconomic system where services linked to information and digitization play a key role. The East and South are still busy, to varying degrees, with catching-up achievements.

Georgescu-Roegen as well is a genius in foreseeing the development of capitalism. Whereas Schumpeter pointed out factors inherent and endogenous to the economic sphere, Georgescu-Roegen contrarily stressed the fundamental relations between mankind's existence and its environmental endowment. His interest is focused on economic development in a world of only limited resources, governed by the physical law of entropy. His economic world doesn't evolve on the basis of unconstrained economic optimism and personal or corporate creativity. It rather runs into an extremely pessimistic scenario of an ecological disaster.

Looking around the globe in these days two development processes, which can be connected with Schumpeter and Georgescu-Roegen, are happening at the same time: A disruptive one based on new technologies like digitalization, robotics and artificial intelligence, creating a new future for working, producing, consuming and fostering economic development. And, a revolutionary negative one, attached to ecological damages, notably caused by CO_2 emissions from fossil fuel use, imperiling climate and nature. In economics these damages are defined as "negative externalities" or "social costs". A growing number of excellent scientific studies in ecology on the impacts of fluid gases on global warming is evidencing a relationship between growing economic activities and environmental imperilment. Such impacts cumulated over centuries, now posing existential threats to animals, plants and humans, as the latest report of the "Intergovernmental Panel on Climate Change" (IPCC) diagnoses in a dramatic wake-up message (IPCC, 2023).

Extreme weather, heat waves and droughts are becoming more and more common. The floodings in Brazil, Spain and Kenya, megadroughts in the Amazon region as well as tropical storms and heatwaves in the year 2024 gave us a foretaste to what may lie ahead for us. It also shows that we are not prepared for dangerous events like these.

That means, more than ever before, we are living in a "risk society", a phenomenon Ulrich Beck, a German sociologist, analyzed in 1986 (Beck, 1986) when the "Cold War", the existential threat of a nuclear conflict, shaped the public discussion. In a "risk society" future is characterized as a socio-economic dimension where positive expectations are still alive shaping society's well-being. But, to a high degree, they are superimposed by negative risks of an existential quality like todays escalating climate warming. "Existential risks" of this kind not only change the stability and flexibility of a complex socio-economic system, they may bring the whole system into a situation of a sudden collapse. Then, "existential risks" touch the system's tipping point (Ord, 2020).

This immense danger attached to climate change has been increasingly recognized worldwide, in the political sphere as well as in civil society organizations. In recent years self-binding agreements have been concluded at global climate conferences to put a stop to global warming and the destruction of natural environment. In the Paris Agreement of 2015, for example, 196 countries committed to the goal of limiting global warming to 1.5 degrees above pre-industrial levels and taking all available measures to achieve this target until 2035.

Which consequences does all that have for economic reasoning elaborating insights and ideas in a Schumpeterian kind of thinking? In which way has the traditional Schumpeterian approach, focusing primarily on technological progress and economic success, to be modified or transformed into a "Post-Schumpeterian" analysis which succeeds in dealing with both sides of today's socio-economic reality, the demand for "economic prosperity" as well as the need for "natural" or "environmental security". Or, more generally formulated: What are the principles of "Post-Schumpeterian Economics" (PSE) combining economics with ecology and joining Schumpeter with Georgescu-Roegen?

These are the first big questions our study intends to answer analytically.

The second big theoretical issue is to ask in which way "Post-Schumpeterian Economics" is able to find solutions for one of the most urgent global challenges in our time, the quest for transforming "brown" into "green" economies. What are the strategies and devices to find a way out of the traditional evolutionary oriented Schumpeterian modes of development, having "brown" economies in mind, into a new "Post-Schumpeterian Era", focusing on future oriented sustainable success in "green" or "clean" economies?

We will deal in detail with both big questions in the first, analytical part of the study, which is authored by **Horst Hanusch**. A change in Schumpeterian thinking has to be initiated. Society's progress in prosperity based primarily on the visionary idea of an unlimited creative process of innovative activities has to be extended and transformed into a "targeted system of development" related both to the traditional Schumpeterian dynamics of innovative growth and the security determined approach to cope with the existential risks and global threats of environmental damages and/ or other percipices (Ord, 2020), which already exist or may come into existence.

We start our analysis outlining the "Principles of Post-Schumpeterian Economics" (PSE). In a first step a short introduction of the original Schumpeterian thinking is given, continued with an overview of "Neo-Schumpeterian Economics" (NSE), an advancement of the original concept. This shall give us an idea concerning the theoretical background of "Traditional Schumpeterianism". We will see that this approach is pursuing "prosperity" mainly as "quantitative growth" in the original context and as "qualitative or evolutionary development" in NSE, focusing on industrialized countries with highly developed mechanisms of structural change. In both versions environmental damages are not regarded. Or, more generally formulated, the "ecological demand" doesn't play a role as a necessary ingredient of a concept which has to define development as a kind of "hybrid process" bringing together economic with natural requirements.

In this part of the study we will also see that there are two constitutional elements determining development in a Schumpeterian system:

(a) The "market or price system" of an economy with its competitive mechanism of demand and supply, being responsible for the allocation and distribution of resources in an efficient and fair way;
(b) the "innovation system" of an economy, driving the dynamic processes of growth and structural change.

In the emergency situation of climate change these two systems have to be changed decisively from a purely "anthropocene" and "brown" orientation to a "post-anthropocene" and "green" intention. For this transformation a number of strategies may qualify, depending on whether the "market price system" or the "innovation system" of an economy is regarded as the starting point of change.

Concerning the transformation of the price system several options are of interest, two more idealistic and a more pragmatic one. Both versions intend to "internalize social costs" into the decision processes of the economic agents.

(1) The first option wants to internalize "social costs" by introducing "true prices". This could be achieved either by striving for a "dedicated evaluation system" in which the economic actors voluntarily include "external effects" in their individual decision processes or, by administrative orders to change the worldwide used System of National Accounts (SNA) respectively. Both alternatives are highly idealistic approaches depicting a way of development which might be characterized as a highly theoretical building frame for a concept of "Evolutionary Post-Schumpeterian Economics" (EPSE).
(2) The second option intends to install an "Emission Trading System" into the market process as the main instrument of "green climate policy". In this more pragmatic procedure the evolutionary characteristics of traditional NSE as well as PSE will be transmitted into a "directed" system, which will then depend

heavily on government specifications concerning the price and quantity of CO_2 emissions as part of the overall market price system.

With regard to the transformation of the innovation system, the first question to be asked is whether the private sector can manage the necessary disruptive change by its own. If not, the helping hand of government has to be taken into consideration. In that context "Green Technology Policy" is generally assessed as an adequate strategy to start and gear a process of transition in the "National Innovation System" (NIS) from "brown" to "green".

Advantages and disadvantages, possibilities and limits of the above mentioned transformational options will be widely discussed in Chap. 2, the theoretical part of the study.

What this study is not interested in, is to deal with a methodological alignment in ecological economics which tries to develop the fundaments of a "green growth" approach replacing the National Account System with an indicator based approach using variables like "national asset base", "policy responses", "socio-economic outcome", and "quality of life" or "environmental productivity" (Sarkodie et al., 2023).

The second part of the study is empirically authored by **Yasushi Hara**. It tries to find out whether and to what degree nations around the world have already entered the "Post-Schumpeterian" path of development. Do they take commitments like the "Paris Agreement" seriously and acknowledge the necessity to employ appropriate measures to set off for a process of future orientation which will integrate material fortune with security of climate and nature, heralding a transformation of development paradigms never experienced before.

Regarding this empirical concern the shift from "brown" to "green" is especially crucial for the group of G-20 countries which are nowadays responsible for 80% of worldwide CO_2 emissions. This group includes different regions of the planet with different levels of national development and represents the industrialized G-7 nations as well as the BRICS countries together with a number of selected developing countries. G-19 group consists of the following member states: Argentina, Australia, Brazil, China, Germany, France, Great Britain, India, Indonesia, Italy, Japan, Canada, Mexico, Russia, Saudi Arabia, South Africa, South Korea, Turkey, the United States and two regional bodies, the European Union and the African Union. And the G-7 group is composed of the following member states: Germany, France, the United Kingdom, Italy, Japan, Canada, and the United States. Whereas the BRICs countries Brazil, Russia, China, India, and South Africa are pooling the interests of emerging nations. These countries comprise two thirds of the world's population and account for most of its economic output. The G-19 group is the most important country grouping making significant statements on climate change at recurring conferences with resolutions and terms of their commitment that go far beyond those of the United Nations. The group was just meeting in Rio de Janeiro (2024) to find effective solutions to stop the increase of global warming. Its members can be considered as the forerunners and opinion leaders to develop a political arrangement to fulfill the quest for a global transformation (Mazzucato et al., 2024).

In summary, the empirical part of the study wants to illustrate whether and to what degree a Post-Schumpeterian System is already on its way in the G-20 countries. Can we observe a development process in these countries, which is already in transition from an "industrial" or "post-industrial" stage towards a "Post-Schumpeterian Era" characterized by a sustainable shift of economic activities from "brown" to "green"?

To cover these questions we concentrate as well on two major issues: Firstly, we are asking whether there exists economic growth simultaneously with a fall of the environmental impact, measured by CO_2 emissions, whereby the growth rate of GDP includes all kinds of growth: substitutive, neutral, capacity expanding or degrading growth. The answer to this question is given by scrutinizing "decoupling", i.e. segregating in absolute terms growth as a combination of its different components and relating it to CO_2 emissions.

This overall view looking at growth and CO_2 emissions, is then expanded with a more "Schumpeterian" point of view looking at "productivity", as the most important element of growth in its relationship to CO_2 emissions.

This analysis is continued by an empirical examination of the innovation process of an economy. Here "green technology" as the transformer and economic driver of a sustainable global development plays the decisive role, either in its already applied version or in a future oriented one documented by "green patents". In this examination we will especially have a look at "green ecosystems" which consist of the "green technologies" and artificial intelligence (AI), as a "general purpose technology", having strong effects on the content, efficiency and smartness of the transformation process.

These investigations are worked out for all member states of the G-20 grouping and for the G-7 economies and the BRICS countries as a separate bloc of nations with different geopolitical interests, to get an idea about the global situation the "Quest for Transformation" is confronted with.

To realize the empirical intentions an "indicator approach" for the variables used is implemented in combination with "cluster analysis" (Jobson, 1992). The target of the cluster analysis is to detect cross-national-(dis-)similarities in the structure and composition of the group of G-20 countries concerning their "state-of-the-art" in being on the way to a "Post-Schumpeterian Era".

Chapter 2
Theoretical Schumpetarian Background: Toward Global Economic Transformation

The following section presents a brief overview of Schumpeterian ideas on economic development, tracing their origin in Schumpeter's work and their subsequent evolution over recent decades into the broader concept of 'Neo-Schumpeterian Economics'. Both the original and advanced versions serve as the building blocks and underpin the principles of a PSE, which seeks to address innovative growth alongside climate change, meeting the global imperative for transformation across both highly and less-developed economies.

We begin with Schumpeter's original concept of progress and prosperity.

2.1 Original Schumpeterian Ideas: Progress and Prosperity

The core of original Schumpeterian thought is articulated in *The Theory of Economic Development* (Schumpeter, 1912). It presents the essential elements of a functioning, progressive capitalism. Creative and visionary entrepreneurs, armed with new ideas to transform the ecosystems of living, consumption, and production, combine that with risk capital to initiate and finance innovations. This process generates dynamic change, producing new goods and services as well as novel combinations of labour, capital, and knowledge in production, thereby creating individual or firm-level success that cumulatively increases the 'Wealth of Nations'.

This vision of development without 'limits of growth' has been observable since the Industrial Revolution. Today, it is exemplified by the terms 'entrepreneurial' or 'technological capitalism', as practised in the US Silicon Valley, with its iconic figures in information and communication technology. When dynamic entrepreneurs such as Jeff Bezos, Bill Gates, Steve Jobs, Mark Zuckerberg or Elon Musk operate within a transnational market supported by necessary risk capital, they generate 'growth engines' or 'techno-capital machines' of remarkable innovation (Andreessen, 2023). A similar dynamic applies in China, where entrepreneurs like

H. Hanusch, Y. Hara, *Innovative Growth and Climate Security*, SpringerBriefs in Economics, https://doi.org/10.1007/978-981-92-1005-3_2

Wang Chuanfu (BYD), Ren Zhengfei (Huawei) and Pony Ma (Tencent) harness creativity and risk-taking to fuel Schumpeterian technological dynamics that foster progress and prosperity (Wang, 2025).

Currently, millions of start-ups worldwide await confirmation of this concept of entrepreneurial spirit, which Schumpeter described as 'the dream or will to found a private kingdom' or 'dynasty for which industrial commercial success is still the nearest approach … possible to modern man' (Schumpeter, p. 93). This drive to conquer, to prove superiority, and the joy of 'creating' a new world characterise the psychology of 'dynamic entrepreneurs' (Fagerberg, 2003).

However, when a dynamic entrepreneur's overwhelming business success translates into political ambition, the figure of the 'oligarch' emerges, wielding both economic and political power (Rushkoff, 2023). This scenario often arises during periods of revolutionary or disruptive technologies, when entrepreneurs with substantial risk capital seek to exploit commercial opportunities by pressuring governments to reduce regulatory oversight.

Today, technologies such as digitalisation, robotics, and artificial intelligence are reshaping the world and providing fertile ground for the Schumpeterian model of success. Yet, these developments may also herald the early stages of societal 'oligarchic elitism'. History demonstrates this tendency particularly in the United States, where economic brilliance has periodically correlated with increasing political influence (Beckert, 2024), as current Silicon Valley trends and the 'robber barons' of the late nineteenth century illustrate.

2.2 Comprehensive Neo-Schumpeterian Economics

In the literature, the original Schumpeterian economic system is referred to as 'Schumpeter Mark I'. It was succeeded by 'Schumpeter Mark II', which encapsulates the central themes of *Capitalism, Socialism and Democracy* (1936). In this framework, large corporations possessing extensive human and financial capital assume the role of 'dynamic entrepreneurs', igniting economic progress.

Both versions experienced a prolonged period of intellectual neglect. Only in the early 1990s did economists increasingly recognise both approaches, 'Schumpeter Mark I' and 'Schumpeter Mark II', gaining prominence in academia and policy. This intellectual trajectory culminated in 'Neo-Schumpeterian Economics' (NSE), enriched with several theoretical elements extensively discussed in the literature (Hanusch & Pyka, 2007a).

Key developments include:

- Emphasising innovation as the principal driver of 'structural change' across industries, shifting the concept of growth from a purely quantitative to a qualitative dimension (Jones, 2002).

- Introducing the concept of the 'National Innovation System' (NIS), comprising diverse actors such as firms, research institutions, policymakers, and consumers (Lundvall, 2005; Nelson, 1993).
- Highlighting the significance of formal and informal technological networks or 'ecosystems' connecting firms, governments, universities, and research institutions (Saviotti & Pyka, 2004).
- Incorporating 'Innovation Economics', which addresses complexity in economic and social relationships, focusing on coordination, networking, mutual learning, cross-fertilisation across knowledge fields, and the development of competences and capabilities.

Despite these advances, NSE remained incomplete as a theory of economic development, primarily focusing on the economy's real sphere (Hanusch & Pyka, 2007b). Technological innovations clearly drive industrial dynamics and growth, but they are neither the sole force nor can industry develop in isolation. Development is accompanied and shaped by novelty and change in the monetary and public sectors as well.

In this institutional context, 'Comprehensive NSE' (CNSE) (Hanusch & Pyka, 2007b) gains significance as a future-oriented theoretical framework. CNSE builds on both the original and Neo-Schumpeterian concepts but prioritises institutional relevance in development. It emphasises the financial and public spheres alongside the real sector, identifying these three pillars as crucial for co-evolutionary dynamics that generate both quantitative growth and qualitative transformation.

The future, in this framework, possesses a historical temporal dimension and remains open to 'creative destruction', ongoing transitions, and unforeseen events, incorporating genuine uncertainty. This applies to all three pillars (real, financial, and public) whose co-evolutionary development varies in prominence across time and countries. Sustaining this process requires the creation and diffusion of a continuous flow of novelties within each institutional domain. This holistic 'innovation fabric' depends on preparatory activities in each sector and specific institutional relationships to maintain and strengthen co-evolution.

For example, the real sector must develop a 'format of resilience' to foster knowledge-driven progress and wealth, achieved primarily through science, research, creative innovation, and parallel investment. The financial sector's role is to support this resilience by forming a close, almost symbiotic relationship with the real economy. Its principal task is to establish a sound financial foundation that enables individuals and firms to pursue innovative, future-oriented activities, even when motivated by speculative interests.

Government and political authorities hold responsibility for inspiring, monitoring, and regulating the long-term relationship between the real and financial sectors. They may also support co-evolutionary development through targeted budgetary and institutional measures, particularly investments in education, health, infrastructure, and science and research.

A concise representation of CNSE's core principles is provided in Fig. 2.1.

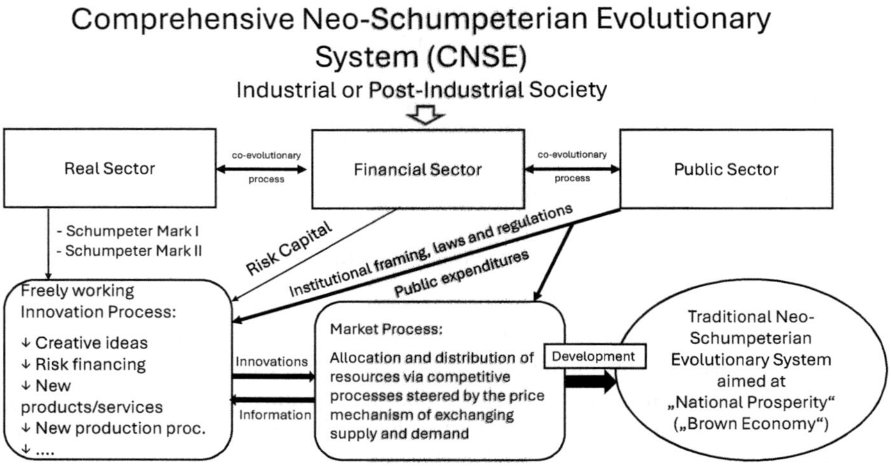

Fig. 2.1 Comprehensive Neo-Schumpetarian Evolutionary System(CNSE)

As Fig. 2.1 illustrates, the CNSE represents a complex framework reflecting the socioeconomic context of an 'industrial or post-industrial society', emphasising either manufacturing sectors or service functions, particularly in finance. The system comprises three institutional pillars (the real, financial, and public sectors) that interact co-evolutionarily. The real sector is largely shaped by the 'innovation process', embedded within an NIS. Dynamic entrepreneurs or start-ups (Schumpeter Mark I), alongside internationally competitive firms (Schumpeter Mark II), develop new products, services, and production processes based on individual or corporate creativity and capability. These actors require risk capital, provided by the financial sector, and a supportive institutional environment, comprising laws, regulations, and public expenditure, offered by the public sector.

These innovations enter the market, triggering a process of 'creative destruction', driven by price and innovation competition, which replaces or complements existing solutions with forward-looking alternatives. This structural change generates, through diffusion and spill-over effects, unforeseen economic opportunities. In a feedback loop, market information returns to the innovation process, consistent with Hayek's concept of 'Wettbewerb als Entdeckungsverfahren' (competition as a discovery procedure) (1969). Ultimately, the market's allocation and distribution mechanisms develop a 'brown economy' scenario focused on the sustained growth of national prosperity. Historically, from an economic perspective, this traditional Schumpeterian approach has proven capable of fostering immense increases in the 'wealth of nations', particularly since the Industrial Revolution (Gordon, 2016).

In summary, CNSE, as an extension of original and Neo-Schumpeterian thought, remains highly relevant for understanding and explaining the economic foundations of modern capitalist economies. However, it has two significant limitations. First, it primarily concentrates on individual nations and their development; transnational issues arise only in discussions of 'international competition and trade'. Global challenges that inevitably affect all countries, such as 'existential global risks', fall outside its scope. Second, the approach neglects 'social costs', negative externalities occurring during development, especially when 'nature' as a global public good is exploited in production and consumption.

In both respects, the global threat and social costs of climate change exemplify CNSE's deficiencies and the urgent need for reform. This necessitates a profound extension of CNSE that fundamentally alters its paradigmatic framework. The pursuit of prosperity and wealth characteristic of 'brown' economies must be reconciled with the ecological imperatives of a severely damaged natural environment. This reconciliation requires 'green' development alternatives within a new paradigm, which we term 'Post-Schumpeterian Economics' (PSE). The following discussion will address this framework.

2.3 Post-Schumpeterian Economics

As previously noted, we are living in an era marked by unprecedented technological transformation and ecological risk. These are not ideological upheavals, but rather structural shifts driven by technological innovation and environmental degradation, both of which increasingly shape our present and future.

On one side, technological disruption (through digitisation, robotics, and artificial intelligence) has become a central concern of contemporary economics. On the other, the ecological crisis, exemplified by accelerating climate change and biodiversity loss, poses systemic risks that challenge the foundations of socio-economic stability. These concerns form the primary focus of ecological analysis.

It is noteworthy that, aside from Nicholas Georgescu-Roegen and Kenneth Boulding, few major economists have seriously engaged with the possibility of nature posing existential threats to human life. Foundational figures such as Adam Smith, Karl Marx, and John Maynard Keynes did not integrate these concerns into their economic frameworks.

Today, however, the notions of economic success and environmental catastrophe can no longer be addressed in isolation within separate disciplines. The standard division of labour, practised in conventional neoclassical and Schumpeterian economics (CNSE), which addresses economic development, and ecology, which focuses on environmental degradation, has become inadequate. Climate change demands an interdisciplinary approach that closely integrates economics and ecology. In this context, existential threats must be embedded within a Schumpeterian dynamic framework, which traditionally remains oriented towards national economic performance.

This requires translating the ecological imperatives of the Anthropocene into a dynamic economic model, transforming the prevailing national development paradigm into a transnational 'green' system. The pursuit of prosperity, characteristic of a nationally bound, carbon-intensive ('brown') economy, must be reconciled with the ecological imperatives of climate change, which transcend national boundaries and entail global consequences.

Accordingly, two seemingly antagonistic dimensions ('economic prosperity', defined as a national and quantitative objective, and 'ecological security', understood as a transnational and qualitative imperative) must be unified. Each must inform and redefine the other within a shared developmental lexicon. In economic terms, climate must be recognised as a public good, one that benefits and is shared by the global community (Enzyklika *Laudato si'*, 2015). Simultaneously, climate change must be conceptualised through the economic category of 'social costs'. Both concepts form the constitutional basis of a 'hybrid' development model in which ecological considerations are translated into economic terms.

This dual definition of development, encompassing both private interests and common social values, challenges the traditional Schumpeterian paradigm, which is inherently one-dimensional. The original framework is centred exclusively on the private sphere of goods and services, subject to property rights, and does not sufficiently account for public goods, social costs, or collective welfare.

To summarise the Post-Schumpeterian approach:

In the face of global existential threats such as climate change, the traditional, one-sided Schumpeterian development model, as represented in CNSE, must be reformulated into a multidimensional trajectory that incorporates two key components:

(a) a transnational dimension, driven by global existential threats;
(b) a hybrid dimension, integrating both private and common goods within a framework of sustainable development.

This multifaceted structure may be termed a 'Post-Schumpeterian System' of development. The corresponding body of theory may thus be referred to as PSE.

2.4 Post-Schumpeterian Transformation

In the following section, we elaborate on how PSE can address the urgent 'Quest for Global Transformation', the transition of economies worldwide from 'brown' to 'green'. Can this global challenge be met with the analytical tools of PSE? What strategies and instruments are available and appropriate for achieving this transformation?

The 'Post-Schumpeterian System', as previously discussed, offers two primary pathways for realising this global transition:

(a) revising the valuation mechanism within existing market price systems, and/or
(b) directing the innovation process of an economy.

The first approach involves internalising the 'social costs' of climate change within the value framework of an economy. The second entails reorienting the objectives of the NIS, shifting its focus from solely 'prosperity and growth' to also include 'climate protection' and 'environmental preservation'.

We begin with the concept of internalisation, which can be divided into two variants: an idealistic and a pragmatic approach.

2.4.1 Internalising 'Social Costs': Idealistic Transformation Strategies

Idealistic strategies are generally categorised under two conceptual frameworks: the 'dedicated system' approach and the 'true costs' approach.

2.4.2 Dedicated System Approach

The most straightforward, albeit idealistic, solution to the transformation challenge would be for all economic agents, both producers and consumers, to voluntarily alter their decision-making orientations and behavioural patterns to significantly reduce their 'fossil footprint'. Particularly within the household and consumption sectors, which are major contributors to climate change, heightened individual awareness could result in measurable reductions in CO_2 emissions, thereby bringing climate neutrality within reach.

However, voluntary climate action in these sectors presents complex methodological issues, well recognised in welfare economics, notably under the theme of 'utility interdependence'. This concerns the explanation of individual decisions involving heterogeneous attributes within a 'philanthropic preference function' (Boulding, 1962).

Historically, scholarship in this area has focused on reconciling 'allocative efficiency' and 'fair distribution' as components of individual utility functions, exploring whether 'social rationality', expressed as altruistic behaviour, can emerge from such conditions (Hanusch, 1972). This question has remained central to behavioural and empirical microeconomics, even receiving Nobel recognition (Kahneman et al., 2019).

In the context of climate change, a new line of inquiry emerges: Can 'self-interest', manifested as 'free riding' in the consumption of common goods, coexist with 'renunciation', understood as the assumption of social responsibility, to foster 'sustainable behaviour'? This would constitute a contemporary form of altruism aligned with ecological and economic imperatives. While theoretical and empirical investigations are still in their infancy, preliminary research has begun (Douglas & Brauer, 2021).

From a Schumpeterian perspective, this model of altruistic sustainability invites scepticism. Such behavioural change would likely result in a contraction of economic output, implying not 'more' in the Schumpeterian sense of innovation-driven prosperity, but 'less' in the classical ecological sense, an idea already anticipated in *The Limits to Growth* (Meadows et al., 1972).

Furthermore, the implementation of altruistic behavioural change becomes increasingly difficult as the number of beneficiaries from 'free riding' grows. Climate change, as a global externality, compounds this challenge. Individuals may feel disempowered, submerged within a vast, transnational anonymity of billions of 'external beneficiaries'. Even when climate protection gains formal recognition due to the existential nature of the threat, effecting meaningful behavioural change at the individual level remains arduous. As the transformation of preferences toward sustainability unfolds on a global scale, individual agency in determining climate outcomes is significantly diminished. If such behavioural change were easily achievable, the climate crisis would arguably not exist.

In contrast, firms in the production sector present a slightly more optimistic scenario. According to the Carbon Disclosure Project (CDP), a London-based non-profit established in 2000, two-thirds of global market capitalisation now reports environmental data (CDP, 2023). However, data reporting alone does not equate to the implementation of strategies that integrate profitability with sustainability.

In practice, climate-related orientations and levels of engagement vary significantly across firms and regions, as our empirical findings will demonstrate. A major impediment is 'path dependency', which individual firms often cannot overcome in isolation. We will return to this issue in our discussion of the limitations and possibilities inherent in a CO_2 trading system. Stimulating and coordinating firms' transformation strategies at the global level represents a substantial challenge for both private management and public governance.

These difficulties partly stem from the implementation structure of the Paris Agreement. The 1.5-degree target, although internationally endorsed, lacks enforceability through environmental law. As a 'bottom-up' framework, it grants individual nations the freedom to determine their own contributions to climate security. In practice, countries, firms, and households assess climate change differently, based on a complex set of economic and political criteria. Among these, the level of economic development plays a decisive role.

Highly industrialised nations, including G-7 members, may perceive stringent environmental regulations as threats to national sovereignty rather than instruments for averting global catastrophe. Meanwhile, countries undergoing industrialisation are unlikely to relinquish the advantages of inexpensive fossil energy, especially when such resources underpin their development strategies. A transition from 'brown' to 'green' development will remain elusive unless wealthier countries commit to, and enforce, international agreements that include financial compensation for less developed nations. Mechanisms such as concessional loans could support this transition. Even if the rationale for such a shift is sound, it remains politically and economically difficult to implement. As Kenya's President William Ruto remarked at the first Africa Climate Summit in September 2023: *'We must go green fast, before industrialising, and not vice versa'* (Bearak, 2023).

In summary, achieving a global transformation requires more than voluntary behavioural change. Economic agents, whether in developed or developing countries, must be persuaded that climate protection aligns with their own self-interest. A promising avenue is the creation of a global value system, standardised through international commitments and operationalised via 'true prices'. These prices would serve as information signals and coercive mechanisms through market forces, shaping individual decisions towards climate-compatible outcomes.

We now turn to an approach that places less emphasis on voluntarism and more on administratively determined 'information ordering' within the Schumpeterian system, where 'true prices' function as the principal driver of transformation.

2.4.3 *Introducing 'True Prices'*

From an economic perspective, the 'true prices' approach is grounded in the recognition that the transformation problem can only be addressed meaningfully if economic agents are persuaded to shift from the free use of climate resources to their protection, acting in their own self-interest. Achieving this shift necessitates the establishment of a new global value system. As noted previously, such a system must be standardised through international commitments, employing 'true prices' as instruments of information and relying on the rules of demand and supply as the coercive force of market competition. The aim would be to orient the market process towards outcomes of prosperity and sustainability, understood as results of an evolutionary economic development.

At first glance, this proposal may appear overly ambitious. However, as will be shown, there are already notable initiatives in scientific research, business, and politics seeking to implement such ideas. It is thus necessary to further examine the 'true prices' approach.

As discussed, inefficiencies arise in the market process when externalities are not incorporated into the valuation and decision-making systems of economic agents. The globally applied valuation system is the System of National Accounts (SNA), first published in 1953. It provides a statistical framework to record the value of economic transactions across countries. The financial data included are based on quantities that the market can price.

This system constitutes the primary informational foundation for global economic activity and decision-making. Despite its universal acceptance and utility, it exhibits significant limitations. Chief among these is its exclusion of externalities, particularly negative ones. As previously argued, it fails to account for 'social costs' and thus ignores the broader economic impact of resource use. Consequently, decisions made in the real, governmental, and financial sectors are based on net market values rather than comprehensive variables that reflect the full costs of production and consumption, including social costs.

As long as this market-oriented valuation system remains in use, a fundamental transformation from a 'brown' to a 'green' economy, one that internalises social costs, cannot be realised. Addressing this requires the statistical internalisation of external effects through the integration of social costs into economic calculations. Without such internalisation, policy efforts to address climate change risk amounting to little more than piecemeal attempts to preserve the existing system. Reforming the current SNA is, therefore, both urgent and of international concern (Stiglitz et al., 2009).

This situation is deeply regrettable. If the current accounting system could be reformed to incorporate a genuine micro- and macroeconomic assessment that includes social costs, a foundation would be laid for a mandatory informational system to guide decision-making across all economic actors. Such a system would operate autonomously, free from national political interference or electoral cycles, and would provide a globally valid computational framework to facilitate the transition to a green economy.

All economic agents (producers and consumers, the state, and the financial sector) would be required to make decisions based on information that reflects the full, 'true' values of their activities. This accounting system would underpin an ecologically informed decision-making framework, applicable in both liberal democracies and authoritarian regimes. On the production side, goods and services would be valued using 'true prices', which would influence supply and demand across markets and guide innovation and investment decisions. Economic actors could not ignore this mechanism without risking their competitive position or even survival.

Firms in the real sector would need to adapt to this expanded valuation system. In the Hayekian sense, they would compete on the basis of price; in the Schumpeterian sense, they would strive for innovation. Either way, firms would find it in their interest to actively participate in the transformation process initiated by the new information and valuation system. Failure to do so could result in lost influence or missed opportunities for leadership in emerging green markets.

Such a system would induce endogenous structural changes across firms, sectors, and regions at both national and international levels, facilitating an evolutionary transition from brown to green economies. The national component would diminish in importance, as the reformed accounting framework would become an international standard based on a taxonomic classification system. This system would track the entire value-creation process, from production to consumption, throughout the lifecycle of products and services in transnational trade, valued from start to finish according to 'true prices'. National corrective policies would then become largely redundant.

Consumers, too, would need to adapt to the new accounting standards. Their behaviour would shift from free-riding to environmentally responsible decision-making. 'True prices' would transparently reveal the dual cost components of goods and services: the proprietary share and the common (environmental) share. This would underscore the significance of nature and climate in all economic activity. If market prices adjust appropriately, the existential risks associated with consumption would also become evident. Consumers would then face pressure to change their preferences and lifestyles, either by replacing brown with green products or by reducing their consumption of emission-intensive goods.

The climate, formerly treated as a free resource, would come to be perceived as a 'meritorious good', embodying protection and security as integral to individual utility calculations that include both private and common interests. Optimising both would become a rational survival and prosperity strategy. Achieving this synthesis may require a transformation in individual consciousness, with far-reaching behavioural and lifestyle consequences. Individuals would, through 'true prices', become economically aware of the damage caused by free-rider behaviour and better equipped to weigh it against the benefits of behavioural change.

These ideas are no longer merely aspirational. In the corporate sector, an increasing number of firms now include social balance sheets within their annual financial statements, highlighting their progress in transitioning from brown to green operations. Multinational companies, in particular, are reorienting their management strategies and aligning their innovation and investment priorities with the Paris climate goals. These changes reflect self-interested corporate reasoning, embodied in codes of conduct that set minimum standards for environmental, social, and governance (ESG) practices. A growing number of public corporations have adopted ESG standards, particularly in sectors such as mobility, food, housing, and agriculture. In these areas, firms recognise the profitability of entering emerging green markets as first movers.

This observation remains pertinent, particularly in light of a recent retreat of the ESG movement. Given its high relevance five years ago, a complete withdrawal now seems unlikely.

Of particular importance in this context is the role of shareholders in shaping corporate behaviour. At annual general meetings, their demands for measurable environmental outcomes, alongside financial returns, represent a potentially powerful mechanism for influencing the policies of companies with high CO_2 emissions.

The influence of multinational fossil fuel producers, especially global oil corporations such as BP, Exxon, Shell, and TotalEnergies, alongside numerous state-owned enterprises, should not be underestimated. Their emerging interest in transitioning from the declining fossil fuel sector to the development of renewable energy sources provides cautious grounds for optimism, despite the continued predominance of profit-driven motives.

In the consumer sector, extensive empirical studies are emerging to quantify the environmental impact of food production (PNAS, 2022). Enabled by advances in data processing, this method, referred to as 'True Cost Accounting' (TCA), offers significant opportunities to expand current knowledge (Nature Food, 2021). A related social movement, 'True Price', has already taken shape. It aims to ensure that products are sold at prices which reflect their full environmental and social costs, thereby fostering a sustainable global economy.

In this context, it is worth noting an experimental initiative recently undertaken by the German food discounter REWE in its Penny shops. The experiment involved displaying two price tags for select food items: one indicating the 'true price' of the product, inclusive of the environmental and social costs of production, and the other reflecting the standard 'brown' price associated with current production methods. The price differential serves to reveal the economic cost borne by nature and climate. This additional information is intended to assist consumers in assessing the environmental consequences of their purchases. If such an experiment is feasible on a small scale, it raises the question of whether it could be extended to all goods and services, in line with the vision advocated by the 'True Price' movement.

The concept of 'ecological conversion' has also reached the financial sector. Central banks in industrialised countries are increasingly integrating ecological assessment criteria into their reporting, often through ESG standards. By offering guidance and recommendations, they seek to influence private investment behaviour, most notably, by encouraging support for ESG-compliant funds (NGFS, 2019).

A parallel development within financial markets is the emergence of 'impact investing'. This movement aims to leverage financial market dynamics to promote climate security. In addition to ESG-oriented investments, it encompasses public campaigns and protests at company annual meetings, all advocating for more climate-conscious corporate strategies.

In the public sector, governments have long employed tools such as Benefit-Cost Analysis, in which social costs are accounted for as 'intangible values' and measured in monetary terms during the evaluation of major public investment projects (Hanusch, 2011). In this respect, the state has acted as an early adopter of value-based accounting and reporting.

International organisations such as the United Nations and the European Union have likewise intensified their focus on climate change. The EU, for instance, has introduced sustainability-related classifications through its Taxonomy Regulation, outlining criteria to assess the environmental sustainability of private investments based on ESG standards. Furthermore, the Disclosure Regulation (2022) mandates transparent reporting by financial market participants on the integration of sustainability considerations into their decision-making processes.

In 2015, the United Nations adopted Agenda 2030 as a global framework for a more equitable and sustainable future. Under the UN Global Compact, private firms have committed to developing innovative solutions to achieve the 17 Sustainable Development Goals. To date, over 190 international companies have signed this agreement (UN, 2023).

Overall, the prospects for introducing 'true prices' may be assessed with cautious optimism, though the challenges remain considerable. A critical precondition for such an 'Evolutionary Post-Schumpeterian' approach is the continued existence of globalisation and extensive transnational trade. Climate change is not a regional or national issue; it is fundamentally global in nature.

In summary, a pricing and accounting system based on 'true prices' would facilitate adaptive resilience and transformation processes within the economy, as illustrated in Fig. 2.2. These changes would be driven by endogenous dynamics. The Schumpeterian evolutionary framework described in NSE would gradually evolve into a model of 'Evolutionary PSE', where both market mechanisms and innovation processes operate largely without distortion, oriented towards the dual objectives of growth and environmental security.

Within this system, markets would allocate and distribute goods and services through an accounting framework based on social values, captured throughout the

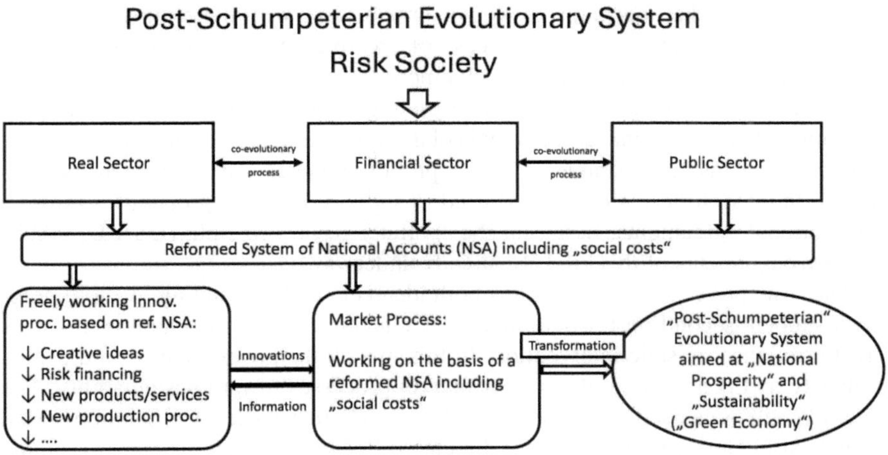

Fig. 2.2 Post-Schumpetarian Evolutionary System

value-added chain in 'social balance sheets' and summarised in a social 'profit and loss account'. These records would inform consumers of the true cost of their consumption choices. Consumers could then opt for 'brown products', characterised by lower production costs but higher environmental damages, or select 'green' alternatives that may be more costly to produce but incur significantly lower environmental impact.

Producers, in turn, would be equipped with the relevant information to guide their innovation and investment decisions. Firms could then choose whether to remain in environmentally harmful sectors or pivot towards greener, higher-value-added alternatives.

In the financial sector, documentation based on 'true prices' would enable more comprehensive assessments of firms. Beyond market profitability, companies could be evaluated on the basis of their environmental performance, moving the focus of ratings towards 'green' success indicators.

Nevertheless, despite the appeal of an 'Evolutionary Post-Schumpeterian' approach, one major concern must be addressed. At the national level, particularly in the consumption sector, this model raises significant issues of distributive justice. The initial implementation of 'true prices' would likely lead to substantial price increases, which would stabilise only gradually. Although such inflation would be largely transitory and not driven by conventional factors, it would require active policy intervention. In this transitional phase, the responsibility would fall more on social policy than monetary policy. Governments would need to provide financial compensation to consumers (so-called 'climate money') to offset the increased costs incurred from paying 'true prices'.

In contrast, the production sector should be capable of managing the transition independently, relying on price signals and competitive innovation. In this scenario, extensive government intervention through subsidies or penalties would be unnecessary. Market mechanisms would furnish firms with the requisite information to initiate a Schumpeterian process of creative destruction and to pursue a dynamic transition towards green development.

At the international level, a key challenge lies in the persistent disparity between wealthy and poorer countries. A global solution would require financial compensation mechanisms, comparable to those proposed under the 'dedicated system' model. Industrialised nations would need to support developing countries through transnational agreements, based on the 'polluter pays' principle (USAID, 2024). Some arrangements of this kind are already underway.

The 'true price' approach remains both idealistic and demanding. A more pragmatic, albeit second-best, solution to the challenge of transformation involves greater reliance on state intervention. In this model, the government would use its authority and economic tools to steer market processes toward sustainability. The free and self-organised development trajectory characteristic of a Schumpeterian system would be replaced by a more directed framework, as Paul Romer envisioned (Romer, 1990), in which both market and state share responsibility for guiding economic transformation.

In such a 'directed economy', governments may choose to intervene in market operations by politically restructuring existing price–quantity relationships across various markets. This approach is already being implemented in many industrialised nations, particularly among the G-7 group, through policies collectively known as 'green climate policy'.

2.4.4 Installing an 'Emission Trading System': 'Green' Climate Policy as Transformation Strategy

'Green Climate Policy' is widely explained in textbooks and numerous articles on climate change (Cullenward & Victor, 2020). It is based on the premise of remedying market failures caused by 'social costs' through policy instruments designed to alter the incentive or activity structures of consumers and/or producers. Typically, this form of climate policy employs 'certificate trading' for CO_2 emissions alongside a politically determined quantity restriction on emissions, which progressively tightens over time. For example, the European Commission, which first implemented such a system in 2005 as the coordinator for EU member states, and the Federal Republic of Germany, as a national executor, both endorse this concept as a market-based approach. The state conceals its dirigisme behind a solution that declares pollution rights a tradable commodity, leaving economic agents to determine the quantity and intensity of use, provided they pay accordingly. Gradually, all economic activities, from production to consumption, and all market sectors concerning individuals, households, and companies fall within this framework.

In addition (or alternatively), tax policy measures attempt to induce behavioural change, such as levying a tax on gasoline consumption, a major polluter. Such fiscal coercion aims to pressure economic agents to switch from high-emission activities to less polluting alternatives.

At first glance, these approaches appear to offer a 'philosopher's stone'; they enjoy strong endorsement in mainstream economics and politics as effective remedies. However, a closer examination, particularly from a Schumpeterian perspective, reveals both minor and significant weaknesses. A few examples suffice here. The trading approach, for instance, often neglects the risks of deception and fraud when state-induced behavioural changes lack stringent controls, which themselves demand extensive bureaucracy. This problem, often termed 'greenwashing', represents a considerable source of misinformation (de Freitas et al., 2020).

From an institutional viewpoint, the trading concept is embedded in a framework dominated by the financial sector, enabling trading activities to detach from real economic conditions and thereby amplify speculative influences.

Conversely, tax policy interventions confront well-known challenges, such as tax avoidance and difficulties in eliciting truthful preference revelation from individuals (Ostrom et al., 2002).

Moreover, both trading schemes and tax policies require long time frames to achieve meaningful effects, if at all. This delay motivates environmental activists, including the 'Fridays for Future' movement, to demand more decisive state intervention through strict regulations and legal prohibitions aimed at securing 'climate security'. Yet, such a stringent political course risks unsettling liberal democracies, with unforeseen consequences for social cohesion. Firstly, it may disrupt the institutional balance between the market and the state. Secondly, illiberal or dirigiste political elements may exploit this tension, mobilising anti-environmental protest movements that decry alleged state overreach enacted in the name of climate protection.

It is also essential to recognise that both trading and tax policies possess a strong geographical dimension. Each country, even within supranational entities such as the EU, may implement climate policies with varying degrees of stringency, influenced by societal, economic, and political factors. However, 'climate and environmental protection' constitutes a global public good, achievable only through collective agreement and efficient, equitable implementation by all states. Unfortunately, the trading approach has largely been treated politically and administratively as a local, regional, or national issue, with insufficient regard for its universal character.

From a Schumpeterian analytical perspective, the principal critique of 'traditional climate policy' lies in its focus on market processes to modify supply and demand decisions as is shown in Fig. 2.3. These instruments rest on the assumption that regulatory interventions in the 'system of relative prices' using a zero-sum strategy (Lundvall, 2005) operate equivalently to spontaneous market price changes.

Do consumers, compelled to pay a price for CO_2 emissions associated with certain goods or services, behave as they would in response to ordinary market price increases? Likewise, do firms subject to a CO_2 tax react as they would to market price competition? The answer is unequivocally no.

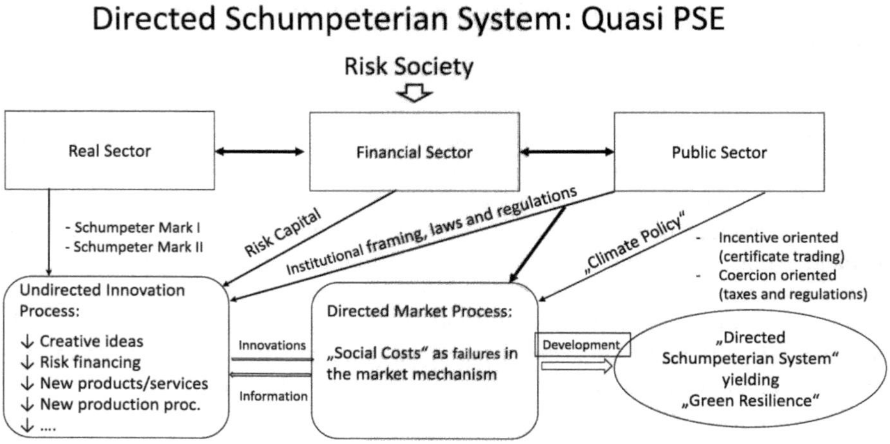

Fig. 2.3 Directed Schumpeterian System

The CO_2 trading system ultimately constitutes only a 'quasi-price system', allowing agents and countries to opt out of the intended transformation. Firms may relocate production to countries with more favourable conditions, and consumers may resist climate policies by voicing opposition in the political arena, fostering general scepticism or even political conflict. This resistance manifests either as an ideological conviction denying climate change or as conservative apprehension about the financial burdens imposed by climate policies. Consequently, state-imposed climate protection risks becoming part of an ecological 'culture war' between supporters and opponents of the environmental movement, with significant repercussions for government action (Mathiesen, 2022). Should politicians increasingly interpret public scepticism as the 'will of the people', democratic processes will prompt corresponding policy adjustments. Climate protection risks losing its primacy and legal standing, as exemplified by Germany's Federal Government 'Climate Protection Act' (Bundesregierung, 2019), to become merely one among many political priorities. This downgrading of climate change is observable not only in Germany but also across most developed countries, notably the United States.

For firms, the current CO_2 trading system preserves geographical freedom of choice: companies may invest in preferred countries, particularly in economies more tolerant of climate-damaging production. Emission-intensive industries retain the option to relocate manufacturing to regions with less stringent climate regulations, especially when comparing developed countries to economies undergoing 'catch-up' development. Ultimately, global GDP may increase without contributing to global climate protection. Indeed, climate change may worsen, as developing countries in the 'Global South', with currently low emissions, may willingly trade 'climate damage' for 'economic growth'. In this scenario, stringent climate policies in industrialised countries could be partly blamed for undesirable global developments.

As a consequence of such potential scenarios, national emissions trading policies must necessarily be combined with a system of ‘climate tariffs’. Otherwise, high carbon dioxide (CO_2) prices in one country will cause so-called ‘carbon leakage’, whereby firms located in countries with high CO_2 costs relocate to jurisdictions with low or no such pricing. For this reason, the European Union introduced the world’s first ‘climate tariff’ in 2023.

‘Climate tariffs’, however, entail certain trade-political risks that may escalate into a ‘trade war’. To prevent nations from pursuing unilateral trade policies that could devastate the transnational trading system, proponents within the EU argue that ‘climate tariff clubs’, with uniform tariffs across member states, could provide a beneficial solution. The establishment of such institutions, however, may prove as challenging as reforming the National Accounting System.

The goal of favouring ecological requirements could, without doubt, be achieved most swiftly and effectively through individual renunciation and acceptance of a shrinking GNP, as advocated by extremist environmentalists and so-called ‘doomsayers’ (Tupy & Pooley, 2023). Their ‘degrowth’ proposal, which is attracting increasing attention, demands not only the complete cessation of high CO_2-emitting activities within the production sector but also a fundamental reduction of the consumption sector’s environmental footprint. Only ‘less’, rather than ‘more’, as suggested by Schumpeterians and so-called ‘cornucopians’ in the climate policy discourse, can ensure the desired sustainability outcomes (Coy, 2023).

We do not intend to engage in an extensive discussion of the degrowth approach here but refer instead to Daniel Susskind’s recent critique, which characterises it as one of the greatest misjudgements in economics and potentially a tragedy in practice (Susskind, 2024). Employing a typical Schumpeterian argument, Susskind contends that growth is not finite but rather an infinite process, provided that sufficient new ideas are generated and applied productively.

In this context, it is noteworthy that, in Japan, an intellectual movement known as ‘ecological Marxism’, inspired by a recently published book by Saito (2023), is gaining public interest. This movement seeks to reconcile Marxist ideals of ethical solidarity with the goal of climate security. Its fundamental premise is that climate change can only be resolved within a shrinking or steady-state economy aligned with the highest ethical and solidaristic standards, taking into account current and future generations. However, from a cornucopian perspective, such ethically based considerations represent an extreme form of ‘escapism’, a flight from the realities characterising the existing global economic order.

Based on the above arguments, ‘green climate policy’, whether implemented through emissions trading or tax instruments, does not necessarily lead to a global transformation from a ‘brown’ to a ‘green’ economy. From a Schumpeterian perspective, such a transition requires more than a politically imposed adjustment of prices and quantities between more and less polluting goods and services. It also demands a transformation of the NIS toward a green growth and development dynamic. This structural change, however, is only implicitly assumed by proponents of green climate policy. The process of transitioning from dirigiste price and quantity controls to a sustainable, innovation-driven growth dynamic remains unexplained and obscure within the emissions trading framework. Technological progress is relegated to the 'black box' of neoclassical economics, and thus its direction and outcomes cannot be predicted a priori, as numerous studies in Schumpeterian innovation economics have demonstrated (Hall, 2013). The result is uncertain: innovation may be stimulated or inhibited. The outcome depends on various factors, including the polluter's economic conditions and the characteristics and future orientations of markets generally.

What can be asserted with confidence is that changes in the system of relative prices alone may enhance an economy's resilience in responding to the climate crisis. Such changes may also alleviate individuals' 'existential fear' by limiting high CO_2-emitting activities. As an adaptation policy implemented through directed or commanded political means, emissions trading may act as a form of 'palliative recovery policy', likely to be effective in a shrinking economy. However, it cannot directly induce sustainable development in the sense articulated by PSE, which defines it as a technology-based, dynamic economic process driven by the creation and diffusion of innovations that reconcile extensive growth with ecological concerns, thereby transforming the economy from 'brown' to 'green'. This objective cannot be fulfilled without explicit changes in factors critical for the green transition. It is not merely the costs imposed on producers and consumers to achieve net-zero emissions that matter, but also the welfare of consumers and profits of firms generated by striving for and establishing climate neutrality. Perceived welfare motivates consumers to pay for climate security, and expected profit guides corporate decision-making and shapes the innovation process, which lies at the heart of a Schumpeterian economy and its dynamic forces (Brett, 2024).

We now turn to consider how governments can influence the innovation process through green technology policy to facilitate the transition from a 'brown' to a 'green' economy, as illustrated in Fig. 2.3.

2.4.5 Innovation Process-Oriented Transformation Strategy: 'Green' Technology Policy

The Schumpeterian literature typically discusses 'technology policy' within the framework of economic prosperity, emphasising wealth creation and national competitiveness (Hanusch & Pyka, 2007b). However, introducing 'climate security' as a parallel priority to economic growth complicates the policy landscape significantly. This dual objective necessitates a 'green' innovation policy that challenges the state to manage considerable complexity. Two principal approaches emerge within this context, both grounded in the NIS and Schumpeter's concept of 'creative destruction': a *Palliative Recovery Policy* and a *Supervised Positive Sum Strategy.*

2.4.6 Palliative Recovery Policy

The first approach, a *palliative recovery arrangement*, aligns conceptually with a 'trading' strategy. It represents a 'green' technology policy primarily addressing market failures, especially CO_2 emissions, while preserving existing economic structures. This strategy is most effective when the state adopts the role of an active investor, initiating and implementing climate change mitigation technologies (CCMT). The policy's scope remains narrow, interpreting 'sustainability' largely as a technological response to air pollution.

This aspect of innovation policy has gained prominence under the concept of the 'entrepreneurial state' (Mazzucato, 2013). Simultaneously, ecological discourse has increasingly focused on 'geo-engineering' (Wagner, 2021), a technical discipline developing projects such as carbon capture and storage or solar radiation management (SRM). Although these innovations remain in early developmental stages and far from large-scale implementation, they deserve closer attention from both policymakers and private sector actors.

The CCMT-envisioned NIS is characterised by partial effects in both economic and ecological terms. It seeks to mitigate the environmental impacts of economic activity without altering the foundational structure of the 'brown' economy. On the contrary, it aims to preserve existing industrial systems and sustain conventional industries and firms as engines of growth. Rather than transforming the system, this approach introduces incremental technological enhancements. Figuratively speaking, CCMT resembles a palliative treatment, alleviating symptoms without curing the systemic 'disease'.

2.4.7 Supervised Positive Sum Policy

An alternative or complementary strategy is the *supervised positive sum policy*, wherein the state intervenes in the innovation process either directly, as a financial risk-taker, or indirectly, as a cooperative political actor. The aim is to initiate and steer the transformation through 'green' technology policy. Here, the state assumes the role of a supervisory actor, responsible for concept development, implementation, and monitoring. See Fig. 2.4 for illustration.Direct engagement may involve the state leveraging its creditworthiness to support innovative start-ups, acting as guarantor or risk investor where private capital is insufficient.

This model has found significant support in Asia, particularly in Japan and China. However, this study focuses primarily on indirect interventions, where government efforts aim to shape producer expectations and encourage shifts from 'brown' to 'green' production through incentives, guidance, and support.

Such measures may include strategic communication, subsidies, or tax incentives that highlight opportunities and facilitate transitions, for instance, resolving managerial or logistical challenges. These policies rest on a broader understanding

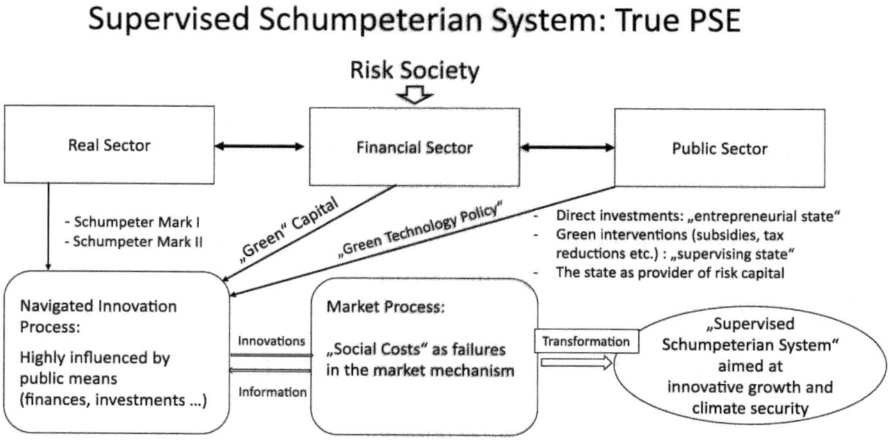

Fig. 2.4 Supervised Schumpeterian System: True PSE

of innovation. The NIS no longer addresses a single issue (e.g., environmental degradation), but fosters a systemic transformation influenced by environmental imperatives and emerging general-purpose technologies such as artificial intelligence (AI).

This reconceptualisation reaffirms the relevance of Schumpeter's notion of 'creative destruction'. Economic progress stems from replacing outdated structures with innovative alternatives. New jobs, industries, and services emerge, potentially supplanting or complementing legacy sectors, however, in a rigorous, disruptive version comprising proprietary as well as common dimensions.

In this *Comprehensive Post-Schumpeterian Innovation System*, the dual objective is to generate 'new growth' while preserving the environment. The public sector's challenge lies, first, in identifying sectors most attractive to private investors; second, in supporting innovation initiatives; and third, in overseeing the process with cooperative and constructive engagement.

Key questions include: Which sectors, industries, or firms are best suited for a growth-oriented yet ecologically conscious innovation process? To what extent should government and public administration supervise this transformation?

One particularly promising sector, increasingly attracting global public and private interest, is clean energy for mobility. This encompasses solar, wind, and hydrogen technologies for energy production, battery storage solutions, and electric vehicles, all designed to reduce reliance on fossil fuels and promote 'clean growth'.

These so-called 'three technologies', often featured in policy frameworks, are integral to building a new ecosystem. This transformation must incorporate developments in digitalisation, AI, and data processing, which can revolutionise operations across the product lifecycle, from design to manufacturing and end-of-life (Siemens, 2022). In the mobility sector, for example, the traditional 'brown' system based on coal, steel, and combustion engines is giving way to a technologically advanced 'green' ecosystem. Here, autonomous vehicles powered by clean energy integrate seamlessly with intelligent infotainment systems. The 'old car' is reimagined as a digitally enhanced device, closer to a smart system than a conventional vehicle.

Within this new ecosystem, AI plays a pivotal role as a general-purpose technology, enhancing efficiency and intelligence across technological domains. While this study does not explore AI in detail, it is worth noting the substantial momentum it has gained globally. Many economists envision a new era akin to the 'Roaring Twenties'. Leading figures such as Demis Hassabis and Yann LeCun argue that AI can accelerate scientific breakthroughs in fields like medicine, climate science, and green technologies, potentially ushering in a golden age of discovery.

On the one hand, AI may help resolve the longstanding 'productivity paradox' constraining contemporary capitalist economies (Brynjolfsson, 1993) by enhancing human productivity and unlocking significant growth potential (Suleiman & Bhaskar, 2023). On the other hand, it may establish the technological foundation needed to reconcile economic expansion with the imperatives of a 'risk society', which increasingly contends with existential threats. From a Post-Schumpeterian perspective, the phrase 'More from Less', as used in Andrew McAfee's (2019) recent work, signals an important shift in this direction.

A Post-Schumpeterian 'green' technology policy thus presents governments with a strategic choice: either to build a comprehensive ecosystem underpinning a fundamentally new NIS or to pursue incremental adjustments within the existing structure. This freedom, however, warrants caution. Countries with technologically advanced 'brown' industries may find disruptive transformation socially and economically destabilising. For instance, Germany's automobile sector currently faces this dilemma. Abrupt structural change could lead to rapid deindustrialisation, widespread job losses, and social unrest. In such contexts, the 'positive sum' outlook may devolve into a 'zero sum' mindset, where perceived gains for some come at the expense of others. As a result, societies in these economies may gravitate towards partial or palliative recovery strategies rather than comprehensive transformation.

Conversely, emerging economies caught in the 'middle-income trap' may find more substantial opportunities for renewal and advancement through a disruptive and comprehensive Post-Schumpeterian development process. Such a strategy could enable them to leapfrog into advanced green technologies and ecosystems without incurring significant sunk costs, allowing a direct transition into a promising 'Post-Schumpeterian Era.'

Although emphasis is placed on the role of the state, the financial sector also plays a critical role in technology-oriented transformation. Both private financial institutions and national central banks can exert considerable influence through green capital initiatives and regulatory frameworks, as demonstrated in the empirical analysis. Given its global integration, the financial sector is well-positioned to support transnational strategies aimed at addressing climate and environmental challenges.

A crucial dimension of transformation concerns the evolving role of the state. A climate-neutral technology policy or innovation strategy, whether partial or comprehensive, fundamentally redefines the government's role within the socio-economic system. The state gains heightened significance in shaping societal decision-making processes and is expected to offer visionary guidance alongside the institutional capacity to direct private-sector innovation towards desired developmental trajectories.

The government thus assumes a dual role: as an inspirer and initiator, providing early-stage support to start-ups and incumbent firms undergoing transformation; and as a coordinating actor, facilitating collaboration between the public and private sectors to restructure the technological landscape. In this capacity, the state becomes a kind of supervisory entity, closely monitoring and managing the interplay between private and public spheres to ensure alignment with societal transformation goals.

This expanded authority and responsibility empower the state to shape future developments significantly. The 'interventionist government,' as described by is redefined as a 'supervising body,' tasked with overseeing the transition from 'brown' to 'green' economies. This reconceptualisation marks a departure from the neoclassical 'market failure' framework and the Keynesian reliance on general public expenditure. While the latter emphasises macroeconomic stabilisation, it does not provide targeted mechanisms for technological change. The Marxist concept of a 'paternalistic government' is also inadequate, being overly idealistic and insufficiently equipped to address the pragmatic challenges of existential environmental threats. Rather, the proposed model resonates more closely with the 'dedicated system' approach discussed earlier.

This shift, from an 'intervening' to a 'supervising' state, applies to both liberal democracies and authoritarian regimes once green technology policy becomes the primary instrument for achieving climate neutrality and positive, value-added growth. The innovation process increasingly reflects a Post-Schumpeterian institutional arrangement, a 'supervised economy' shaped by two primary forces: the visionary efficiency of government and the innovative capacity of the private sector.

These dynamics have significant institutional implications. In authoritarian regimes, the state often serves as the dominant pillar in the socio-economic framework, with the market functioning as a liberalising force to introduce flexibility and dynamism into economic processes. In liberal democracies, the market system must accept the visionary state as a guiding actor, capable of overcoming path dependencies and structural inertia. Here, the state assumes responsibility for guiding the economy towards sustainable futures, akin to a supervising educator.

Thus, the transformation from a 'brown' to a 'green' economy is shaped less by ideological preferences tied to governance forms, whether authoritarian or democratic, and more by rational, knowledge-driven decision-making across public and private sectors. Both governance models may converge towards a collaborative institutional framework, a Post-Schumpeterian system, where vision, creativity, technological capacity, and coordination become decisive in achieving transformative objectives. Or, they may even generate a "one world totalitarian state" as Peter Thiel is suspecting when the mighty forces of AI, dominating the future, will clash with the existential risks characterizing today's global situation (Douthat, 2025).

Nonetheless, a pressing concern arises within this emerging Post-Schumpeterian era: the issue of efficiency in both public and private sectors. Do governments possess the foresight and institutional capabilities to manage future-oriented transitions? Does the market exhibit the intellectual and technological strength to realise government-initiated visions?

These questions remain unresolved. With regard to governmental capacity, a form of geo-economic competition centred on green technology policy appears to be intensifying. Consider the United States' Inflation Reduction Act (IRA) of 2022, China's 14th Five-Year Plan, and the European Union's Green Deal (2021), which is now evolving into the Clean Deal Industrial Plan. All these programmes require a high level of governmental efficiency, alongside substantial public subsidies to initiate and support green innovation in the private sector.

On the private side, critical questions also emerge. Do NISs possess the flexibility to align with governmental directives? Do public guidelines encourage private firms to engage in high-risk, long-term projects? Does government support risk fostering inefficiencies or a 'self-serving mentality' within the private sector? Moreover, could a government-led supervisory approach to innovation policy evolve into a form of planned economy, echoing Hayek's caution in *The Road to Serfdom* (Hayek, 1944)?

Such questions underscore potential drawbacks of a state-led supervisory approach to technological development. A deeper concern involves the potential for the private sector to use its economic power to gain disproportionate political influence (Rushkoff, 2023). In characterising Schumpeterian entrepreneurs, the term 'oligarchic elitism' captures the risk of economic and political interests merging in technologically advanced economies. Under a supervisory state, oligarchic enterprises may seek not only to influence public policy but to supplant parts of the public sector entirely (Slobodian and Tarnoff, 2026). A common strategy involves portraying bureaucracy as a barrier to future-oriented innovation.

The United States offers a pertinent example. As early as the 1960s, Harvey Leibenstein highlighted the need to enhance public administrative efficiency (Leibenstein, 1966). More recently, a movement known as 'Technopoly', described by Postman (1993), has emerged, advocating the subordination of all social and cultural life to technological imperatives. A comparable entrepreneurial posture was evident in China when Jack Ma, founder of Alibaba, challenged the authority of the state and was swiftly silenced.

Currently in the United States, a group of private-sector actors, reportedly tolerated by government under the label DOGE (Department of Government Efficiency), is pushing for aggressive administrative reform. Their actions appear to go beyond a legitimate quest for administrative efficiency, instead initiating a process of technocratic encroachment into state sovereignty. This development raises concerns about the emergence of a 'techno-political' movement, one that seeks to reframe deep structural reform as 'visionary' progress, echoing libertarian critiques of the so-called 'deep state' (Tuccille, 1970). Whether such a radical reinterpretation of governance, driven by libertarian ideals and justified by appeals to efficiency and innovation, can endure remains uncertain (Slobodian, 2025).

2.5 Summary of the Theoretical Part and Concluding Remarks

This chapter has outlined a comprehensive theoretical foundation for what is termed PSE. This framework extends Joseph Schumpeter's classical theory of innovation-driven growth into a global context, one increasingly shaped by the existential challenge of climate change. The central concern is how economies can transition from 'brown' systems, reliant on fossil fuels, to 'green' systems that are ecologically sustainable, while retaining the dynamic forces of progress, prosperity, and innovation that characterise capitalist development.

The argument begins with Schumpeter's original vision. In his early work (*The Theory of Economic Development*, 1912), Schumpeter emphasised the role of visionary entrepreneurs who combine new ideas with risk capital to initiate dynamic innovation processes. This mechanism of 'creative destruction' has historically generated significant wealth since the Industrial Revolution and remains evident today, from Silicon Valley to China's technology sector. However, this model also entails risks: when economic success translates into political power, oligarchic tendencies may emerge, particularly during disruptive technological revolutions such as digitalisation, robotics, and artificial intelligence. Schumpeter's later writings (*Capitalism, Socialism and Democracy*, 1942) shifted focus from individual entrepreneurs (Schumpeter Mark I) to large corporations capable of institutionalising research and development (Schumpeter Mark II). Both versions affirm that innovation is central to capitalist dynamism.

Subsequent developments in economic thought gave rise to NSE, which expanded upon these ideas by emphasising the systemic and institutional context of innovation. NSE introduced key concepts including structural change, NIS, technological networks and ecosystems, as well as complexity, learning, and capability building. However, it initially concentrated on the 'real economy', overlooking the roles of finance and public governance. This limitation led to the emergence of CNSE, which situates innovation within a co-evolutionary system comprising three pillars: the real sector, the financial sector, and the public sector. Each pillar generates novelty, interacts with the others, and jointly drives growth through both quantitative expansion and qualitative transformation. CNSE highlights historical openness, uncertainty, resilience, and continuous feedback loops between innovation, finance, and governance. Nevertheless, it remains largely national in scope and does not explicitly engage with global existential threats such as climate change.

Herein lies the rationale for PSE. Unlike its predecessors, PSE explicitly incorporates the global ecological dimension. Climate is treated as a global common good, and climate change is framed in terms of social costs that must be internalised within economic reasoning. The challenge is to reconcile two seemingly contradictory imperatives: the pursuit of prosperity (a quantitative, national objective) and the need for ecological security (a qualitative, transnational necessity). PSE reconceptualises development as a hybrid process that integrates private and public goods, technological progress, and international cooperation within a new model of sustainable transformation.

To enable this transformation, the theoretical framework identifies two overarching levers: reforming the market price mechanism to internalise ecological costs, and redirecting the innovation process towards green trajectories.

The first strategy (internalising social costs) can take two primary forms. The most idealistic is the *'dedicated system'* approach, in which consumers and firms voluntarily alter behaviour to reduce their fossil footprint. However, global anonymity, path dependence, free-riding, and misaligned national incentives render this unlikely to succeed. It may also result in reduced output, echoing the concerns of the *Limits to Growth* debate. A more robust alternative is the *'true prices'* approach, which proposes reforming the global SNA to integrate externalities and social costs into all pricing and accounting mechanisms. This would establish a universal and mandatory information system, compelling all economic actors (consumers, producers, financial institutions, and governments) to make decisions based on comprehensive ecological valuations. While ambitious, elements of this approach are already emerging, including ESG reporting, impact investing, the EU taxonomy and disclosure regulations, social balance sheets, consumer-facing true-cost pricing experiments, and commitments under the UN Agenda 2030. Nonetheless, significant challenges remain, including transitional inflation, intra- and international distributional justice, and the requirement for a functioning global trade system.

The second strategy involves traditional climate policy tools such as emissions trading schemes and carbon taxes. These instruments seek to adjust relative prices to account for pollution. While widely adopted (e.g., the EU Emissions Trading Scheme) and grounded in mainstream economic theory, one has to criticize them as partial and fragile from a Schumpeterian perspective. They risk fostering greenwashing, speculative detachment, and excessive bureaucratisation. Their success is contingent on national implementation, raising concerns about carbon leakage and trade disputes. Fundamentally, they operate as politically directed quasi-price systems and may provoke backlash or cultural resistance. Moreover, they fail to guarantee a transformation of the innovation system, as technology remains treated as a black box used in neoclassical models. Such instruments may address symptoms of climate change but are unlikely to trigger a self-sustaining, green transformation.

By contrast, green technology policy targets the innovation engine directly. Two variants are identified. First, a *palliative recovery policy* seeks technical solutions, such as carbon capture or geoengineering, that reduce emissions while preserving existing brown infrastructures. This approach is partial and limited in scope. The more promising alternative is the *supervised positive-sum policy*, in which the state assumes the role of vision-setter, coordinator, risk partner, and monitor, steering the NIS towards green trajectories. This does not imply replacing markets, but rather guiding entrepreneurial energies, financial flows, and innovation ecosystems toward sustainable directions. Key domains include clean energy production and storage, electrified mobility, and particularly the integration of artificial intelligence as a general-purpose technology capable of accelerating discovery and productivity.

Implementation may vary by context: developed economies with established industries may favour gradual adjustments to avoid deindustrialisation, while emerging economies may leapfrog directly into green systems. Both private and public finance play a critical global role in supporting these transitions.

This supervised economy model necessitates a redefined role for the state. Rather than acting purely as an interventionist or paternalistic authority, the state becomes a *supervising actor*, fostering and monitoring transformative innovation while enabling entrepreneurial initiative. Both liberal democracies and authoritarian regimes, albeit through different modalities, may converge toward this model in their pursuit of climate-neutral development. However, risks remain. Government efficiency is not assured, over-planning must be avoided, and there is a danger of techno-oligarchic capture, wherein powerful firms may attempt to shape or dominate the public agenda. Preventing such distortions is as critical as fostering innovation.

In conclusion, while market-based strategies (e.g., internalisation through pricing, taxes, or trading) remain relevant, they are insufficient to drive a genuine transformation. These approaches may shift consumer incentives and relative prices, but they do not reliably restructure the innovation system. In contrast, a green technology policy, embedded in open global trade and cooperation, presents the most promising avenue for a positive-sum transformation. PSE thus centres on the alignment of a supervising state, a responsive private sector, and a global financial system, all guided by true-cost information and targeted innovation strategies. Collectively, these forces can enable the co-evolutionary transition from brown to green economies.

Various interpretations exist in the literature regarding how technological progress might serve as the foundation for organising the political future of economies. These include the *entrepreneurial state* approach (cf. Mazzucato, 2013) or the *interventionist state* rooted in the political tradition of Karl Polanyi (1944). This study does not seek to engage in a detailed comparative discourse. Rather, it promotes the notion of a *supervising state* whose actions are embedded within a Post-Schumpeterian conception of development. Schumpeter himself, having acknowledged the role of government in capitalism in his later work (Schumpeter, 1942), would likely have supported such an approach.

This concludes the theoretical part of the study. The subsequent section will address the empirical dimension.

Chapter 3
Empirical Illustrations—G-20 Countries in Transition

3.1 Introduction

This chapter is structured as follows. First, the dataset and statistical methodology are introduced. This is followed by an analysis of two core transition metrics: the decoupling of economic growth from CO_2 emissions, and the effectiveness of green transformation measured by productivity relative to emissions. The next section investigates National Innovation Systems (NISs) in the context of green technological transition. The empirical analysis concludes with a discussion of green finance. All computations are conducted for the G-20 as a whole, with focused analysis of the G-7 and BRICS economies.

3.2 Data Set and Statistical Methods

To examine the transformation pathways of the G-20 countries, this study constructs a multi-dimensional dataset derived from leading international sources. Indicator selection is guided by the Post-Schumpeterian framework outlined in Chap. 2, aiming to capture the co-evolution of economic, environmental, technological, and financial systems. Core economic indicators, including GDP growth and total factor productivity (TFP), are sourced from the World Bank and the Penn World Table (Feenstra et al., 2015), respectively. Environmental performance is assessed using CO_2 and total greenhouse gas emissions, drawing data from the World Bank and the World Resources Institute.

To analyse the dynamics of NIS, the study incorporates indicators of both current and forward-looking green technological capacity. These include renewable energy deployment from the International Renewable Energy Agency (IRENA), electric vehicle (EV) sales from the International Energy Agency (IEA), and green patent

H. Hanusch, Y. Hara, *Innovative Growth and Climate Security*, SpringerBriefs in Economics, https://doi.org/10.1007/978-981-92-1005-3_3

activity (Y02 classification) from the United States Patent and Trademark Office (USPTO). The financial dimension is assessed using data on climate-related financial policy, green debt issuance, and the carbon intensity of bank lending, with data drawn from the International Monetary Fund (IMF). A detailed list of indicators, data sources, and temporal coverage is provided in the Appendix.

The Friedman test (Friedman, 1937), a non-parametric test for repeated measures, is employed to assess the statistical significance of each indicator within its respective pillar. Given the national-level aggregation of data, this test is appropriate for identifying dependencies among indicators. Only indicators that reject the null hypothesis are retained in the final analysis.

These indicators are then used in combination with hierarchical cluster analysis (see Jobson, 1992) to identify structural similarities and differences across national socio-economic systems, with an emphasis on future orientation. The cluster analysis seeks to group countries based on structural coherence, while maximising inter-cluster heterogeneity. This involves calculating distance measures between countries based on the standardised indicators, thereby identifying clusters with the highest internal homogeneity and greatest inter-group divergence. As Härdle and Simar (2007) explain, cluster analysis seeks to build homogeneous groups from heterogeneous multivariate data, ensuring that within-group similarity is maximised while between-group differences are accentuated.

The analytical procedure begins by treating each country as an individual cluster. A distance matrix is constructed based on the selected attributes. Countries exhibiting the smallest distances are merged into new clusters. This process iterates, with distance recalculated at each stage, until all countries are grouped into a single cluster.

To identify the optimal number of clusters, all indicators are first standardised to a $[-1, 1]$ scale. The analysis then employs hierarchical clustering using Ward's method. The Duda–Hart stopping rule is applied to determine the ideal number of clusters. This involves examining the Je(2)/Je(1) ratio and the pseudo T-squared statistic. Following standard practice, the optimal clustering solution is defined as that which features a low Je(2)/Je(1) ratio alongside a high pseudo T-squared value, indicating meaningful separation among clusters.

While the G-7 countries are subjected to an independent sub-cluster analysis, the same approach is not applied to the BRICS group. With only five members, the sample size is too small to support a statistically robust cluster analysis; minor data variations would unduly influence the results. Consequently, the positioning of BRICS countries is interpreted within the broader G-19 cluster framework. This approach provides a more reliable contextualisation of the individual BRICS economies within the larger group of major economies, highlighting their distinctive profiles without resorting to statistically unstable classifications.

3.3 Growth and CO_2 Emissions: The De-Coupling Issue

The first empirical topic addresses a concept that has attracted significant attention in the literature on green transformation: the issue of 'decoupling', which explores the historically persistent link between economic growth and environmental degradation (Haberl et al., 2020). As economies expand, they typically increase their consumption of natural resources, such as fossil fuels, water, and minerals, while generating more waste and pollution. This process often results in environmental damage.

Decoupling seeks to weaken or break this correlation, enabling economies to grow without a corresponding rise in environmental impact. It is typically framed as 'absolute decoupling', which occurs when economic output increases while environmental impacts decrease in absolute terms. This scenario represents the sustainability ideal, where economic activity no longer imposes harm on ecosystems, resources, or the climate.

3.3.1 G-19 Countries

This section examines the current status of absolute decoupling across the G-19 countries. The analysis uses data on CO_2 emissions and GDP per capita growth, presented in Figs. 3.1 and 3.2.

Figure 3.3 presents the results of a hierarchical cluster analysis of the G-19 countries, based on two variables: the growth rate of gross domestic product (GDP) and CO_2 emissions per unit of GDP (PPP-adjusted). The analysis uses Ward's method, which minimises total within-cluster variance. The x-axis displays the L2-squared dissimilarity measure, where larger distances indicate greater dissimilarity between clusters.

To determine the optimal number of clusters, the Duda–Hart test was employed. This test compares the variance of a group when divided into two clusters versus remaining as one. The Je(2)/Je(1) ratio indicates the aggregate variance of the two clusters relative to one; lower values suggest a preferable division. The pseudo T-squared statistic measures the distinctiveness between clusters, with higher values indicating clearer separation.

The test results suggest that three clusters offer the most balanced configuration. The Je(2)/Je(1) ratio for three clusters is 0.2187, with a corresponding pseudo T-squared value of 14.29. Although additional clusters yield lower Je(2)/Je(1) values, the decline in pseudo T-squared values suggests reduced separation, confirming that three clusters provide an optimal balance between compactness and distinctiveness.

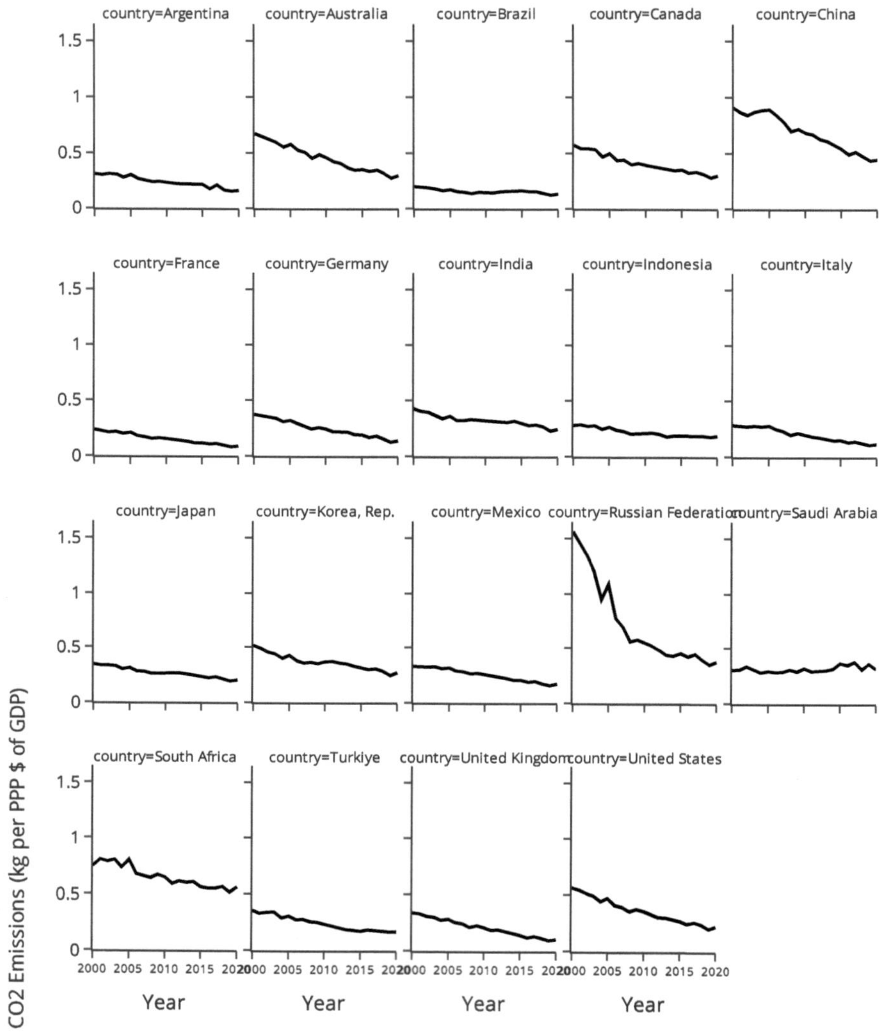

Fig. 3.1 CO_2 emissions (kg per PPP $ of GDP)

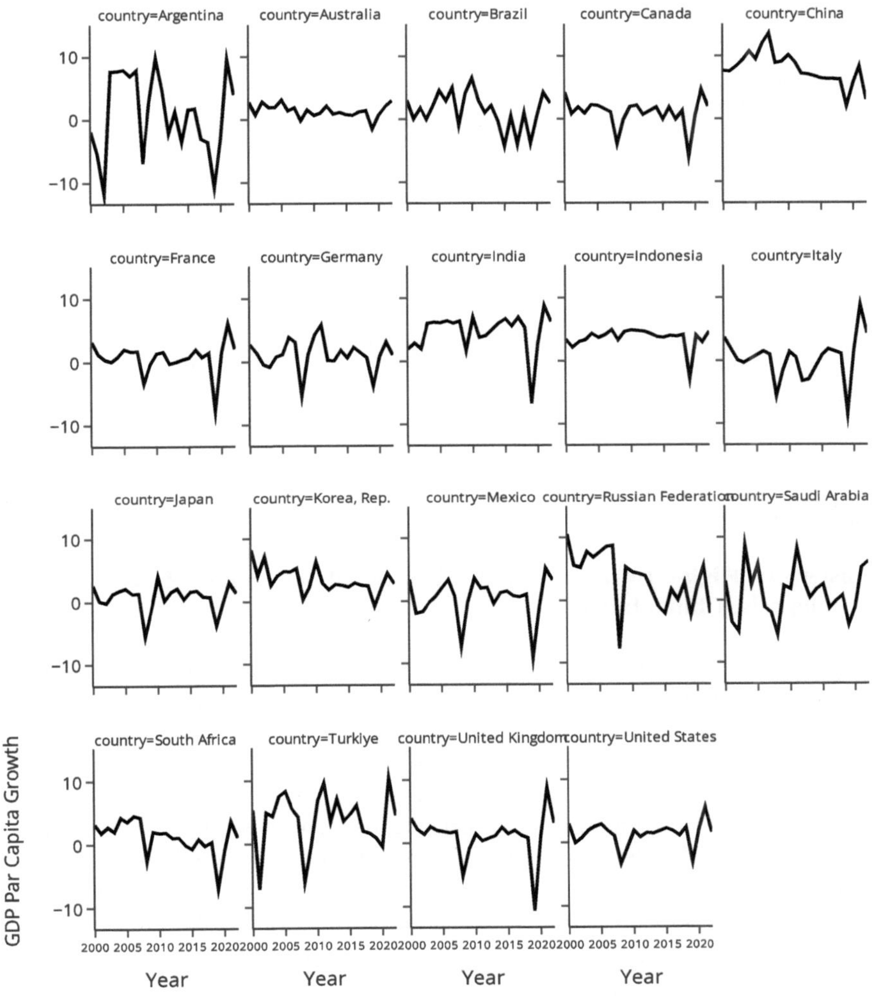

Fig. 3.2 GDP par capita growth

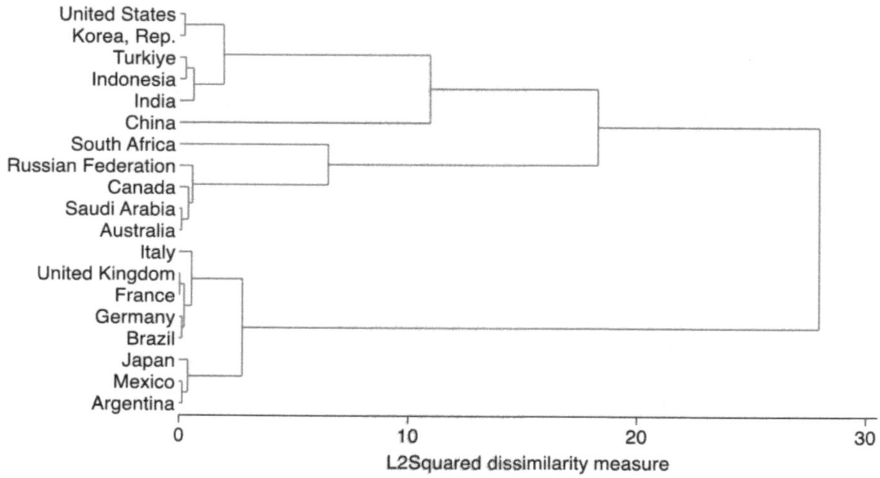

Fig. 3.3 Dendrogram for absolute decoupling

Cluster 1: High-Growth Emitters (United States, South Korea, Turkey, Indonesia, China, India)

This group includes countries experiencing high GDP growth, though CO_2 emissions vary considerably among them. The United States appears to be undergoing a process of reindustrialisation, while the others may be engaged in catch-up industrialisation. Both trends contribute to elevated CO_2 emissions. These countries face significant challenges in balancing economic growth with sustainability, as their industrial sectors are likely driving increased energy demand and emissions. However, a shift from traditional industrialisation, conceived in the Schumpeterian sense, towards a Post-Schumpeterian 'green' transformation could provide a path forward. A later examination of patent systems and the development of green technologies may reveal which countries are progressing towards this new trajectory.

Cluster 2: Carbon-Intensive Resource Economies (South Africa, Russia, Canada, Saudi Arabia)

This cluster comprises resource-dependent economies with moderate GDP growth and relatively high CO_2 emissions per unit of GDP. Their emissions profiles likely stem from the energy-intensive nature of resource extraction and processing. Continued dependence on fossil fuels presents an obstacle to achieving absolute decoupling in these economies.

Cluster 3: Advanced Decouplers (United Kingdom, France, Germany, Japan)

These highly industrialised nations exhibit lower CO_2 emissions per unit of GDP, likely due to their adoption of cleaner energy technologies and more stringent environmental regulations. While their GDP growth rates are relatively modest, they have successfully decoupled economic growth from emissions. This reflects a more sustainable, though less dynamic, development model.

In conclusion, the clustering of G-19 countries illustrates the divergent economic and environmental trajectories among them. The first cluster includes economies grappling with the environmental costs of rapid growth. The second comprises resource-intensive economies that must address their dependency on fossil fuels. The third represents advanced economies that have achieved substantial reductions in emission intensity. These countries have shifted focus from growth-centric models to prioritising economic stability, aligning more closely with the philosophy of 'degrowth' or 'palliative recovery policy' than with a Post-Schumpeterian 'positive-sum strategy'.

3.3.2 Closer Look at the G-7 Transformation Paths

While the analysis of the G-19 reveals broad geopolitical patterns, a focused cluster analysis of the G-7 countries, based on GDP growth rates and CO_2 emissions per unit of GDP (PPP), provides a more nuanced perspective on the diverse transformation strategies pursued by highly industrialised nations. The Duda/Hart test identified an optimal solution of four clusters, revealing distinct transition archetypes even within this advanced group. The resulting clusters are:

Cluster 1: Canada, United States
Cluster 2: France, United Kingdom
Cluster 3: Italy
Cluster 4: Germany, Japan

This grouping underscores that the path towards a Post-Schumpeterian system is not uniform. Rather, it is shaped by national industrial histories, resource endowments, and policy choices, each aligning with the theoretical transformation options outlined in this study.

Cluster 1: The North American Resource-Intensive Growth Model (Canada, United States)
This cluster is characterised by relatively high economic growth and slower decoupling of growth from CO_2 emissions. The higher emissions intensity arises from expansive geographies, reliance on road and air transport, and, in Canada's case, a resource-intensive economic structure. While both countries are advancing in green innovation, their transformation is driven by a blend of Schumpeter Mark I and II dynamics (entrepreneurial and corporate innovation), now guided by substantial public investment. The U.S. Inflation Reduction Act exemplifies this supervised push. This strategy aligns with a *Supervised Schumpeterian System*, albeit from a more emissions-intensive starting point, focusing on developing green industries to compete with, rather than immediately displace, the old.

Cluster 2: The European Post-Industrial Decouplers (France, United Kingdom)
France and the United Kingdom exhibit moderate growth and significantly lower CO_2 emissions per unit of GDP. This decoupling reflects long-term deindustrialisation, transitions to service-based economies, and early adoption of clean energy, particularly nuclear power in France. Their trajectory aligns with a *Directed*

Neo-Schumpeterian System, wherein enduring climate policies and regulatory frameworks, partly shaped by the EU, have constrained emissions. This approach represents a successful form of *palliative recovery policy*, effectively reducing emissions without yet triggering a surge in green-led growth.

Cluster 3: Italy's Unique Transitional Position
Italy's emergence as a single-country cluster highlights its distinct transitional path within the G-7. It neither reflects the high-growth, high-emission model of Cluster 1, nor the effective decoupling observed in Clusters 2 and 4. Structural challenges, such as an industrial sector dominated by small and medium-sized enterprises (SMEs) and prolonged periods of low growth, contribute to this position. Italy's status suggests a transformation path marked by inconsistency, where neither state-supervised technological change nor market-driven greening has yet taken firm root.

Cluster 4: The Industrial Transformers (Germany, Japan)
Germany and Japan, both advanced manufacturing economies, face the complex task of transforming historically emissions-intensive industrial bases. Their strategy represents a textbook case of a *Supervised Positive Sum Policy*, with governments actively supporting green technology development and guiding leading automotive and manufacturing sectors towards a green ecosystem (e.g., EVs, hydrogen technologies). Their prolific output of green patents, as discussed in the G-19 analysis, confirms their central role as innovators. Their path involves a deliberate reinvention process that balances industrial competitiveness with the substantial sunk costs of their existing economic structures.

In sum, the G-7 cluster analysis demonstrates that even among advanced economies, the global transformation is proceeding along divergent paths. Rather than converging on a single model, G-7 countries map onto the theoretical options introduced in Chap. 2. North America harnesses economic dynamism in a supervised transition; the UK and France illustrate both the achievements and limits of a regulatory-led model; Germany and Japan exemplify the technological reinvention of industrial economies; and Italy reflects a complex and less consolidated transition. This diversity reinforces the study's central thesis: the shift to a Post-Schumpeterian era will be shaped by the co-evolution of NISs, market dynamics, and state intervention.

3.3.3 Divergent Paths of the BRICS Nations

In contrast to the G-7, which, despite internal variations, represents a relatively cohesive bloc of advanced economies, the BRICS nations display greater heterogeneity in their efforts to decouple economic growth from CO_2 emissions. As evidenced in the G-19 cluster analysis (see Fig. 3.3), the BRICS do not form a unified group. Instead, they are distributed across multiple archetypes of growth and emissions profiles, reflecting divergent starting points and transformation challenges.

China and India fall into the first cluster, marked by high GDP growth alongside substantial emissions challenges. Their shared trajectory of rapid industrialisation and economic convergence distinguishes their challenge from that of post-industrial G-7 countries. For these nations, the key task is to develop green economic structures concurrently with continued industrial expansion, rather than to retrofit an existing mature economy.

By contrast, the Russian Federation and South Africa are grouped in the second cluster, defined by economic dependence on resource extraction and fossil fuel exports. Their transformation is constrained by structural reliance on carbon-intensive assets. Unlike Germany and Japan, whose challenge lies in modernising industrial systems, Russia and South Africa face the more foundational task of diversifying away from a carbon-based resource economy, a distinct form of path dependency.

Brazil's position is notably distinct within the BRICS group. Its emissions profile is shaped more by land-use change and agriculture than industrial output. This renders conventional metrics, GDP growth, and industrial emissions less effective in capturing Brazil's decoupling dynamics. Consequently, Brazil does not fit neatly into the established industrial archetypes, further fragmenting the BRICS narrative.

In summary, while the BRICS acronym carries geopolitical significance, it obscures profound structural divergence in green transformation trajectories. The bloc includes high-growth industrialisers (China and India), resource-dependent economies (Russia and South Africa), and structurally unique cases (Brazil). In contrast to the G-7's common foundation of advanced industrialisation, the BRICS paths are not only distinct from the G-7 but also from one another. This divergence further supports the conclusion that the transition to a Post-Schumpeterian system will be uneven, shaped by diverse national conditions rather than a singular model.

3.4 Productivity and CO_2 Emissions

National productivity is a key determinant of long-term economic development, serving as a core measure of competitiveness and genuine economic growth.

3.4.1 G19 Countries

A hierarchical cluster analysis was conducted on the G-19 countries using three indicators: (i) CO_2 emissions per capita, (ii) total greenhouse gas emissions, and (iii) Total Factor Productivity (TFP) as a proxy for economic productivity. The Duda–Hart test indicated that the optimal solution consisted of twelve clusters, illustrated in the dendrogram in Fig. 3.4. This fine-grained classification underscores the heterogeneity of economic and environmental profiles within the G-19. For analytical

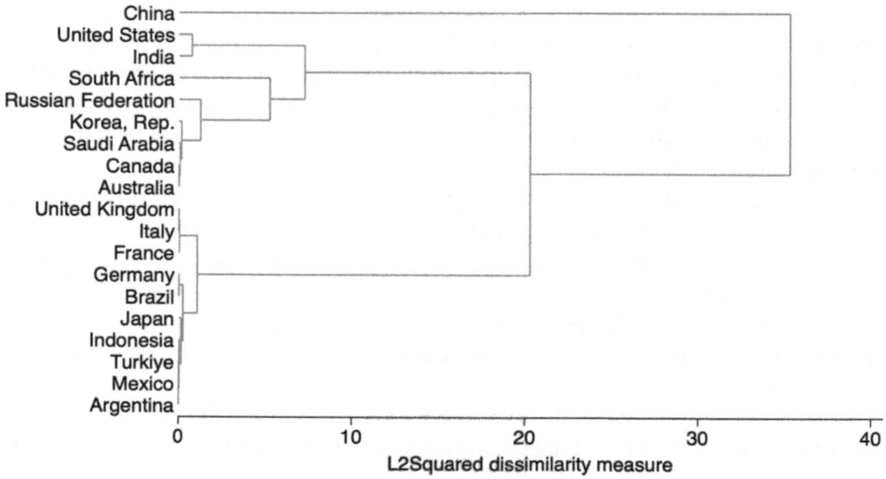

Fig. 3.4 Dendrogram for productivity and CO_2 emissions

clarity, the twelve clusters are synthesised into several archetypes, each reflecting distinctive patterns.

Cluster 1: Indonesia, Turkey, Argentina, Mexico
Cluster 2: Japan
Cluster 3: Germany, Brazil
Cluster 4: Italy, United Kingdom, France
Cluster 5: Australia, Canada
Cluster 6: Saudi Arabia
Cluster 7: South Korea
Cluster 8: Russia
Cluster 9: South Africa
Cluster 10: India
Cluster 11: United States
Cluster 12: China

3.4.1.1 Mega-Emitters: United States and China

A key finding is the distinct categorisation of the United States (Cluster 11) and China (Cluster 12), each forming a separate cluster. Their unique positioning reflects their exceptional roles in the global economy. Both countries exhibit extremely high total greenhouse gas emissions, indicative of their economic scale. However, their productivity profiles diverge markedly. The United States displays one of the highest TFP levels among advanced economies, coupled with an energy-intensive economic structure. China's emissions are primarily driven by rapid, manufacturing-based growth, but its TFP remains below that of the most advanced nations. Although both are mega-emitters, their differing levels of productivity and efficiency justify their separate classifications.

3.4.1.2 Heterogeneous BRICS Nations

The analysis highlights the heterogeneity among BRICS nations, which are spread across multiple clusters. India (Cluster 10) resembles China in terms of high emissions driven by population and economic growth, yet its TFP is significantly lower. Russia (Cluster 8), a resource-dependent economy, shows an emissions profile heavily influenced by the energy sector, alongside a relatively low TFP. South Africa (Cluster 9) is similarly carbon-intensive, relying heavily on coal, which results in high emissions relative to its economic size. Brazil's inclusion in the same cluster as Germany (Cluster 3) is noteworthy. While their TFP levels differ considerably, the statistical similarity in emissions may stem from Brazil's significant land-use change emissions compared with Germany's industrial base.

3.4.1.3 Archetypes of Advanced Industrial Nations

The advanced industrial nations, particularly the G-7, form several distinct clusters. France, the United Kingdom, and Italy (Cluster 4) constitute a coherent group, characterised by high TFP and relatively low total and per capita emissions. This reflects long-standing structural reforms and stringent environmental policies. Australia and Canada (Cluster 5), both resource-rich economies, also exhibit high TFP but higher emissions than their European counterparts. Their geographic and resource profiles contribute to these differences. Japan (Cluster 2) and South Korea (Cluster 7) form individual clusters due to their distinct industrial structures. Both are high-TFP, technology-driven economies with manufacturing-intensive sectors and limited natural resources, leading to unique emissions patterns.

3.4.1.4 Emerging Industrial Economies

Cluster 1 includes Indonesia, Turkey, Argentina, and Mexico, emerging economies in earlier stages of industrialisation, with TFP levels below those of advanced nations. Although their total emissions remain moderate, these countries face the shared challenge of balancing economic development with future emissions constraints. This analysis reveals the substantial heterogeneity within the G-19 in terms of productivity and emissions. The unique positions of the United States and China, the internal diversity of the BRICS, and the differentiated strategies of advanced nations all highlight the necessity of a tailored, multifaceted approach to global climate mitigation, one that accounts for each country's economic and environmental context.

3.4.2 G-7 Nations Analysis

Following the G-19 analysis, this section focuses on the Group of Seven (G-7) nations. A cluster analysis, using the same three indicators (CO_2 emissions per capita, total greenhouse gas emissions, and TFP), yielded three optimal clusters according to the Duda–Hart test. Despite their relative homogeneity, the G-7 countries exhibit three distinct archetypes based on the interplay between economic productivity and environmental impact.

Cluster 1: Japan and Canada—Nations with Unique Industrial and Resource Structures

Japan and Canada form a cluster that reflects shared characteristics and challenges, despite differing economic histories. Japan is a high-TFP economy known for its energy efficiency, a necessity stemming from its resource scarcity. Nevertheless, its emissions remain significant due to a large manufacturing base. Canada, also high in TFP, relies heavily on its vast natural resources and expansive geography, resulting in higher emissions relative to population size.

Although their development paths differ (industrialisation in Japan versus resource dependency in Canada), both countries occupy a middle ground in emissions, falling between the European cluster and the high-emission United States. This suggests that geographic and historical factors impose distinct constraints and opportunities on their respective transitions toward a post-Schumpeterian economy.

Cluster 2: Core European States—A Model of Balanced Transition

Italy, the United Kingdom, France, and Germany comprise a coherent cluster distinguished by high TFP and relatively low emissions. These nations have achieved this balance through long-term industrial restructuring, increased use of renewable energy, and EU-wide environmental policies.

Their per capita emissions are among the lowest in the G-7, positioning them as a model of 'balanced transition', where productivity and sustainability advance together. This cluster exemplifies the concept of a 'Directed Neo-Schumpeterian System', wherein transformation is actively steered by comprehensive policy frameworks.

Cluster 3: The United States—The High-Productivity, High-Emission Outlier

The United States forms a standalone cluster, reflecting its unique economic and environmental profile within the G-7. It has the highest TFP and, by a substantial margin, the highest total greenhouse gas emissions. These outcomes are products of its vast economic scale and energy-intensive industrial base.

This profile indicates that, despite its economic efficiency, the magnitude of the U.S. economy presents significant decarbonisation challenges. The American model of transformation may be characterised as Schumpeterian, relying heavily on technological innovation alongside regulatory interventions to address climate change.

3.4.3 BRICS Countries as a Special Feature

Shifting the analytical focus from the advanced economies of the G-7 to the major emerging economies of the BRICS bloc reveals a landscape marked by profound structural diversity. The comprehensive G-19 cluster analysis based on total factor productivity (TFP) and emissions, presented in Fig. 3.4, offers clear evidence of this heterogeneity. In that analysis, the five BRICS countries are dispersed across five distinct clusters, an indication that, in terms of the core relationship between economic productivity and environmental impact, they do not form a cohesive group. This section examines the specific profiles of each BRICS country, as revealed by the classification.

The analysis identifies China (Cluster 12) and India (Cluster 10) as unique 'developing mega-emitters', each forming a standalone cluster. This reflects their exceptional scale and distinct developmental challenges. While both contribute significantly to global emissions, their economic structures differ markedly. China exhibits the profile of a manufacturing-led superpower with rapidly advancing TFP, where emissions stem largely from its vast industrial base. India, by contrast, remains at an earlier stage of industrialisation, characterised by lower TFP and emissions driven by a different mix of economic activities and population size. Their separation into individual clusters confirms that a singular 'emerging giant' model cannot adequately capture their divergent trajectories.

The Russian Federation (Cluster 8) and South Africa (Cluster 9) occupy another category, each forming its own cluster as a 'carbon-intensive, resource-dependent economy'. Their transformation pathways are shaped by a deep reliance on fossil fuel extraction: oil and gas in Russia, coal in South Africa. This structural dependence results in high emissions relative to TFP, presenting decarbonisation challenges distinct from those faced by manufacturing-based economies.

Brazil (Cluster 3) presents a unique case, being grouped with the industrial powerhouse Germany. This unexpected classification underscores the complexity of emissions accounting. While Germany's emissions stem predominantly from its industrial sector, Brazil's are largely attributable to non-industrial sources such as land-use change, deforestation, and agriculture. Despite substantial differences in TFP and economic structure, their grouping highlights the importance of disaggregating emissions sources when assessing transformation challenges.

In summary, an analysis grounded in productivity and emissions fragments the BRICS bloc into highly individualised profiles. Unlike the G-7, which clusters into archetypes based on uniformly high TFP, the BRICS encompass a wide spectrum: a rising technological superpower, a populous developing economy, two resource-dependent states, and an agro-economy influenced by land-use dynamics. This fragmentation reinforces the central argument that country-specific, rather than bloc-based, approaches are essential for understanding and navigating the global Post-Schumpeterian transformation.

3.5 National Innovation Systems in 'Green' Transformation

This section examines the green transition of National Innovation Systems (NIS) in two parts.

First, it analyses the current state of green transformation, focusing on 'green technologies' already implemented across G-19 countries. Special attention is given to four key technological domains, interpreted as a form of 'green ecosystem': EVs, batteries, clean energy, and, treated as a quasi-green technology, artificial intelligence (AI). This selection aims to provide a representative snapshot of the present state of NIS development across different national contexts.

Second, the analysis expands to include 'green innovations', technologies documented in patents but not yet commercialised, which signal future potential in climate change mitigation technologies (CCMT). This includes one-dimensional technologies such as carbon storage and disposal. A cluster analysis is again conducted to determine whether cross-country similarities exist.

3.5.1 Current National Innovation Systems: Applied 'Green' Technologies in G-19 Countries

This section investigates the development of applied green technologies, specifically clean energy, batteries, EVs, and AI as a general-purpose technology, within the NIS of G-19 countries. These technologies form a cohesive 'green ecosystem' aimed at both expanding productive capacity and reducing carbon emissions. Technologies focused solely on emission reduction, such as hydrogen or biofuels, are excluded. This analysis offers an initial insight into both past developments and the current state of the Post-Schumpeterian transition, centred on NIS. The results are derived from a cluster analysis.

The dendrogram in Fig. 3.5 presents a cluster analysis of G-19 countries based on three key indicators: the share of electricity generation and capacity from clean energy sources, and EV sales. The analysis identifies four distinct clusters, each representing different patterns in green technology adoption.

Cluster 1: Specialised and Uneven Adopters (Canada, Brazil, Saudi Arabia, and China)

This cluster comprises countries either in the early stages of green technology adoption or following divergent energy strategies. Canada and Brazil, for example, rely heavily on hydropower, giving them a high share of renewable energy in electricity generation, yet they exhibit relatively slow EV market growth. Saudi Arabia remains closely tied to its petroleum-based economy, with both renewable energy and EV technologies still nascent. China, while rapidly expanding its EV market, continues to generate a significant portion of electricity from coal, resulting in a lower overall share of renewables.

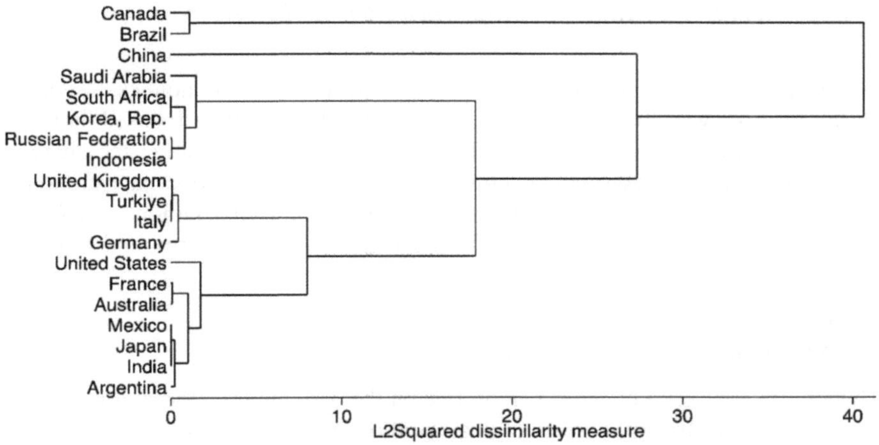

Fig. 3.5 Cluster analysis for the development of applied green technologies

Cluster 2: Fossil-Fuel Dependent Transitioners (Russian Federation, Indonesia, South Africa, South Korea)

This group includes countries with a high dependence on fossil fuels and a gradual shift towards green technologies. Russia and Indonesia maintain strong reliance on oil and natural gas, and EV adoption remains limited. South Africa and South Korea have initiated transitions toward renewable energy and EV deployment; however, the pace remains modest, reflecting the ongoing significance of traditional energy sources.

Cluster 3: Comprehensive Green Adopters (United Kingdom, Turkey, Italy, Germany, United States, and France)

Countries in this cluster have made substantial progress in adopting green energy technologies. The United Kingdom and Germany, for example, have developed extensive wind and solar capacity alongside significant growth in EV adoption. Italy and Turkey, influenced by European Union policies, have accelerated their transitions to renewable energy. The United States and France also demonstrate robust developments in both renewable energy capacity and EV markets, indicating a strong commitment to green transformation.

Cluster 4: Cautious Adopters and Strategic Outliers (Argentina, India, Japan, Mexico, Australia)

This final cluster consists of countries exhibiting slower adoption of renewable energy and EV technologies. India and Argentina continue to depend heavily on coal and oil, despite some expansion in renewable capacity. Japan, while advanced in renewable energy development, retains a strategic emphasis on nuclear power. Mexico and Australia show considerable reliance on fossil fuels, and their EV markets remain underdeveloped compared to other advanced economies.

3.5.2 Green Technology Adoption Patterns in G-7 Nations

To further examine the transition dynamics among advanced economies, a separate cluster analysis was conducted on the G-7 nations. This analysis focused on tangible outcomes of green technology adoption, using three indicators: the share of renewable energy in electricity generation, the share in electricity capacity, and EV sales. The Duda–Hart test identified an optimal two-cluster solution, revealing a primary divergence in strategic approaches to greening the energy and transport sectors:

Cluster 1: Canada, Germany, Italy, United Kingdom
Cluster 2: France, Japan, United States

This grouping offers a nuanced perspective on the ongoing transformation, indicating that national strategies are diverging based on legacy energy systems, industrial policy, and market characteristics.

Cluster 1: Policy-Driven and Balanced Adopters (Canada, Germany, Italy, United Kingdom)
This cluster includes countries that exhibit a more balanced and policy-integrated approach to green technology adoption. Germany, the United Kingdom, and Italy, operating under a common European policy framework, have made sustained efforts to expand renewable capacity, particularly in wind and solar energy, while concurrently developing robust EV markets. Their progress appears systematic, reflecting long-term political commitments to decarbonisation across multiple sectors.

Canada, although geographically and economically distinct, aligns with this cluster due to its extensive hydroelectric resources. This natural endowment affords it a high baseline share of clean energy, aligning it with the policy-driven renewable strategies of its European counterparts. Together, the countries in this cluster exemplify a model where deliberate policy, whether shaped by regional integration or natural advantage, has resulted in consistent, comprehensive adoption of green technologies across the energy and transport sectors.

Cluster 2: Strategic Specialists and Market Giants (France, Japan, United States)
The second cluster is more heterogeneous, comprising countries whose transitions are defined by unique national specialisations or market scale, rather than by a balanced green portfolio. France's energy profile is dominated by its longstanding reliance on nuclear power, which provides the bulk of its low-carbon electricity. This positions it on a distinct technological pathway compared to the renewable-centric approach of Cluster 1.

The United States exemplifies the 'market giant' archetype. Although the share of renewables in its overall energy system has historically been lower, recent policy interventions, such as the Inflation Reduction Act, have triggered rapid growth in both EV sales and renewable installations. Its transition is marked by large-scale acceleration driven by market forces and public subsidies, rather than by incremental, long-term policy development.

Japan, a longstanding leader in industrial and automotive technologies, represents another specialised pathway. Its pioneering role in hybrid vehicles and continued investment in alternative technologies such as hydrogen have shaped a unique trajectory. This focus may have slowed the uptake of fully EVs and moderated the pace of renewable integration relative to European counterparts in Cluster 1.

The divergence into these two clusters within the G-7 suggests a more complex reality than a simple 'leader–laggard' dichotomy. Cluster 1 exemplifies integrated, policy-led development towards a balanced green technology ecosystem. In contrast, Cluster 2 highlights distinctive national strategies: technological specialisation (France, Japan) and the influence of market scale (United States). These findings support the view that the transition to a post-Schumpeterian economy is inherently variegated, shaped by national history, industrial structure, and the chosen mechanisms for managing structural change.

3.5.3 Green Technology Adoption in BRICS Countries

An analysis of applied green technologies, specifically renewable energy deployment and EV adoption, further underscores the heterogeneity within the BRICS bloc. The G-19 cluster analysis (Fig. 3.8) distributed BRICS nations across three of the four identified clusters, revealing a broad divergence in their NIS and technology adoption strategies. This contrasts with the G-7, where, despite strategic variation, all members operate from a higher baseline of technological and industrial capacity.

China again presents a dualistic and paradoxical profile. It falls into the first cluster, reflecting its position as the world's largest and most dynamic EV market, a direct result of a state-supervised industrial policy designed to secure dominance in a strategic sector. However, this rapid progress in transport coexists with an energy system still heavily reliant on coal, situating China as both a global leader in green technology and a major emitter of fossil-based energy.

Brazil, also in the first cluster, illustrates a different form of specialisation. Its electricity mix benefits from vast hydropower resources, providing one of the cleanest grids in the G-19. This natural advantage offers a strong foundation for decarbonisation. Nonetheless, Brazil lags significantly in transport electrification, with EV adoption still at an early stage. Its transition is therefore uneven, advanced in legacy power generation but slow in embracing new technologies.

In contrast, the Russian Federation and South Africa are placed in the second cluster, characterised by fossil fuel dependency and a slow transition trajectory. In both cases, deep structural reliance on oil, gas, and coal has created substantial path dependencies. These structural constraints result in considerable inertia, impeding progress in renewable energy adoption and EV penetration. Their classification as slow adopters reflects the formidable challenge of transforming economies still centred on extractive industries.

India is situated in the fourth cluster, which comprises countries at an early stage of green technology adoption. Like China, India remains heavily dependent on coal. However, unlike China, it has not yet established leadership in applied green technologies such as EVs. As a populous and rapidly developing country, India faces the dual challenge of meeting rising energy demand while initiating a green transition from a relatively low baseline of technological maturity.

In summary, green technology adoption across the BRICS nations is defined by fragmentation rather than convergence. The bloc includes a paradoxical leader (China), a hydropower-rich nation with sectoral imbalances (Brazil), two fossil-fuel-dependent laggards (Russia and South Africa), and a rising power at the outset of its transition (India). This diversity of pathways underscores that there is no unified 'BRICS model' for building a green NIS. Instead, each trajectory is shaped by a distinctive combination of industrial policy, resource endowments, and developmental context.

3.6 Future National Innovation Systems: 'Green' Patents

This section analyses the 'green' patent activities within the G-19 countries, followed by a focused examination of the G-7 nations and the BRICS economies.

3.6.1 'Green' Patents Analysis for G-19 Countries

The dendrogram presented in Fig. 3.6 depicts a cluster analysis of G-19 countries based on their engagement with green patent innovation, as classified under the Y02 scheme. This includes categories such as Y02A (adaptation to climate change), Y02B (buildings), Y02C (capture and storage of greenhouse gases), among others. The cluster patterns allow for a broad classification of countries into four distinct groups, each reflecting varying levels of commitment and strategic focus on green technology development.

Cluster 1: Global Innovation Leaders (United States, Japan, South Korea, and China)

This group comprises nations that demonstrate the highest levels of innovation in green technologies. Their close proximity in the dendrogram indicates considerable similarity in patenting activity across the Y02 classifications. The United States and China, in particular, are leading innovators in energy-related technologies (Y02E), including energy production, distribution, and transportation. Japan and South Korea exhibit strong innovation in transportation (Y02T) and waste management (Y02W). Collectively, these nations have established themselves as central

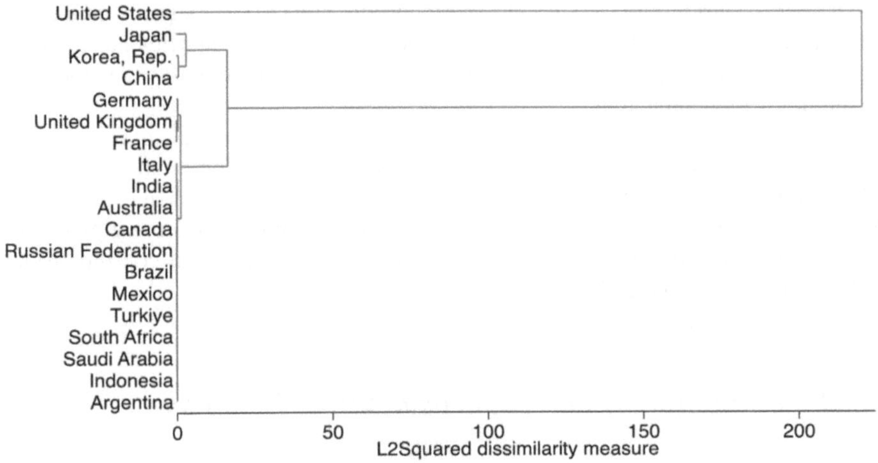

Fig. 3.6 Cluster analysis for Y02 green patents

contributors to global sustainable innovation through extensive engagement across diverse sectors.

Cluster 2: European Innovation Leaders (Germany, United Kingdom, and France)

The second cluster includes European countries recognised for their advanced environmental policies and sustainability agendas. Although their overall patent volumes are lower than those in Cluster 1, they have achieved leadership in areas such as climate adaptation technologies (Y02A) and building energy efficiency (Y02B). Germany is particularly active in smart grid technologies (Y04S), which facilitate the integration of renewable energy into existing infrastructure. These countries exemplify a targeted and policy-driven approach to technological innovation for sustainability.

Cluster 3: Moderate and Diversifying Innovators (Italy, India, Australia and Canada)

The third group encompasses developed and emerging economies. These countries exhibit moderate levels of green patent activity across multiple sectors, without any single nation emerging as a dominant innovator. India, for instance, has shown growth in renewable energy and waste management technologies, while Canada and Australia contribute in areas such as wastewater treatment (Y02W) and agriculture (Y02P). This group reflects a steady, though less intensive, engagement with sustainable technological development.

Cluster 4: Innovation Laggards and Technology Followers (Russia, Brazil, Mexico, Turkey, South Africa, Saudi Arabia, Indonesia, and Argentina)

The fourth group includes nations that demonstrate relatively low levels of green patent activity. While countries like Brazil and Mexico show emerging potential in areas such as agriculture (Y02P) and energy production (Y02E), significant barriers remain to scaling green technologies. Consequently, these countries are likely to depend on technology transfer from more advanced economies to develop their green innovation capacities.

In summary, the cluster analysis reveals significant disparities in green patent activity across the G-19. The United States, Japan, South Korea, and China lead global innovation efforts, while European nations such as Germany, the United Kingdom, and France maintain a strategic focus on sustainability. Emerging economies, including India and Brazil, exhibit incremental progress but continue to lag behind the innovation leaders.

3.6.2 Future Innovation Capacity in the G-7 Nations

An analysis of forward-looking innovation capacity, measured through green patent activity, reveals a clear, tiered hierarchy within the G-7. Unlike the variation observed in applied technologies, the G-7's NIS appear stratified into three distinct echelons. As indicated in the cluster analysis (Fig. 3.6), G-7 countries are not consolidated into a single group; instead, they are dispersed across the top three clusters, allowing for a nuanced understanding of their respective innovation strengths.

At the highest tier are the United States and Japan, both categorised as 'Global Innovation Leaders'. Their inclusion in the top cluster, alongside China and South Korea, confirms their pivotal role in green technological development within the G-7. The United States demonstrates broad and high-volume patenting, particularly in foundational energy technologies (Y02E), driven by a dynamic innovation ecosystem with substantial public investment. Japan's position is sustained by its robust industrial base, with notable strengths in transportation (Y02T) and waste management (Y02W). Together, these nations define the technological frontier within the G-7.

The second tier comprises Germany, the United Kingdom, and France, grouped as 'European Innovation Leaders'. Though their patent volumes are lower than those in the first cluster, their innovation systems are advanced and strategically focused. Germany leads in smart grid technologies (Y04S), while the group collectively excels in climate adaptation (Y02A) and building energy efficiency (Y02B). Their innovation profile reflects a mature, policy-driven approach to sustainability, integrating long-term environmental goals with technological advancement.

Italy and Canada form the third tier, categorised as 'Moderate and Diversifying Innovators'. These countries exhibit consistent, though less intensive, green patent activity. Their innovation profiles are broader and less specialised, with Canada contributing significantly to resource-related sectors such as wastewater treatment (Y02W), and Italy maintaining a generalist portfolio. Their trajectories suggest incremental progress rather than leadership in green innovation.

In conclusion, the future-oriented innovation landscape of the G-7 is stratified. At the top are the United States and Japan, followed by the strategically specialised

European core, and finally, the steady contributors, Italy and Canada. This tiered structure has important implications for geo-economic competition, indicating that leadership in the green economy will be distributed rather than concentrated, with different nations driving innovation in distinct domains.

3.6.3 Innovation Profiles of the BRICS Countries

The green patent cluster analysis (Fig. 3.6) reveals a pronounced hierarchy among the BRICS nations, contrasting sharply with the more consistent innovation levels found within the G-7. The BRICS countries are dispersed across multiple clusters, underscoring a significant internal disparity in green technological development.

China emerges as a clear 'Global Innovation Leader', included in the first and most advanced cluster alongside the United States, Japan, and South Korea. This classification affirms China's status as a leading force in green innovation, with notable strengths in energy and transport technologies. Its NIS is no longer merely catching up but is now shaping the global green transition.

India falls within the third cluster as a 'Moderate Innovator', grouped with countries such as Italy and Canada. While not yet among the top tier, India's consistent patent activity suggests a broadening and strengthening innovation capacity. It is positioned as an emerging player in green technology, though it continues to trail the global frontrunners.

In contrast, Brazil, the Russian Federation, and South Africa are classified in the fourth cluster as 'Innovation Laggards'. These countries display low levels of patenting across most green technology domains. Their limited innovation capacity indicates that progress in sustainable technologies will likely depend on the importation and adaptation of technologies from more advanced economies, rather than domestic innovation.

In sum, the BRICS bloc exhibits a marked innovation gap. China leads with global-level capacity, India demonstrates steady progress, and the remaining members are positioned on the periphery of the green innovation landscape. This internal divergence presents challenges for coordinated action and underlines the asymmetries within the bloc regarding readiness for the green transition.

3.7 Green Finance

This final section of our empirical analysis examines the financial sector's contribution to the green transformation. Using cluster analysis, we assess three indicators:

1. Climate-Related Financial Policy Index (CRFPI): Measures the development of climate-related financial policies in each country.

2. Green Debt: Assesses the volume of green bonds and sustainability-related debt issued by governments and firms.
3. Carbon Footprint of Bank Loans: Represents the greenhouse gas emissions associated with banking sector lending.

We begin with the G-19 economies.

3.7.1 Green Finance Analysis in the G19 Economies

The cluster analysis groups the G-19 countries into four clusters, illustrated in Fig. 3.7. Each exhibits distinct characteristics:

Cluster 1: Emerging, State-Driven Green Finance Systems (China, Saudi Arabia, Russia, Mexico, etc.)
These countries demonstrate expanding green finance initiatives, driven primarily by state-led efforts. Large economies such as China and Russia are advancing financial-sector greening, although the uptake of green debt instruments remains uneven across this group.

Cluster 2: Dynamic, Market-Led Financial Hubs (United States, United Kingdom, India, South Africa, etc.)
This cluster features economies with highly active green financial sectors. Countries such as the United States and the United Kingdom lead in issuing green bonds and promoting sustainable finance through developed capital markets.

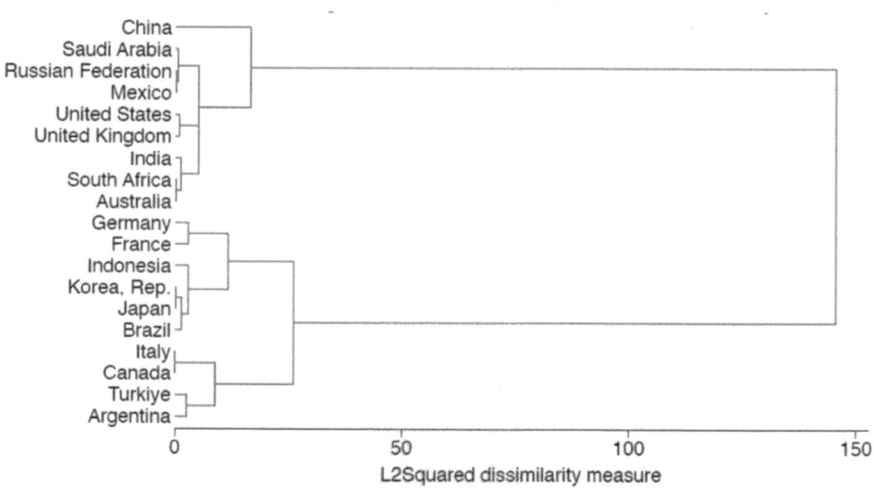

Fig. 3.7 Dedrogram for green finance

Cluster 3: Technologically Advanced with Uneven Financial Greening (Indonesia, South Korea, Japan, Brazil, etc.)
Although these countries are technologically advanced or advancing, their progress in greening the financial sector varies. Inconsistencies in industrial structures and policy adoption rates contribute to divergent outcomes in green debt development and emissions reduction in bank lending.

Cluster 4: Slow Adopters of Green Finance (Canada, Turkey, Argentina, etc.)
Countries in this cluster lag in climate-related financial policy adoption and have made limited progress in expanding green debt markets or reducing the financial sector's carbon footprint.

In summary, the clustering reveals substantial variation in the development and implementation of green finance across the G-19. These differences reflect diverse national priorities, institutional structures, and stages of policy integration.

3.7.2 G-7 Dynamics in Green Finance

We apply the same analytical framework to the G-7 countries, using the CRFPI, green debt volume, and the carbon footprint of bank loans. The Duda–Hart test does not indicate a statistically robust separation among the G-7 based on these indicators. This lack of strong clustering suggests that G-7 economies do not form sharply distinct groups in their approach to green finance.

Nonetheless, the data weakly support a two-cluster solution, offering a useful interpretive framework. This division mirrors a long-standing distinction between market-led and state-influenced financial systems.

Cluster 1: Market-Led Financial Hubs (Canada, Italy, United Kingdom, United States)
This cluster includes primarily Anglo-Saxon economies characterised by deep, mature capital markets. The United Kingdom and the United States, home to globally dominant financial centres, lead in issuing green bonds and deploying market-based green finance instruments. Their CRFPI scores typically reflect policies prioritising transparency, disclosure, and private capital mobilisation. Canada, with a financial system structurally aligned to market principles, fits this pattern. Italy's inclusion, though less intuitive, implies that, according to these indicators, its financial sector exhibits stronger similarities with this market-oriented group than with more state-directed models. This cluster's greening strategy relies primarily on the scale and dynamism of its capital markets.

Cluster 2: State-Influenced and Bank-Centric Systems (France, Germany, Japan)
This cluster features economies where the state and banking sector maintain a more interventionist role. Germany, for example, channels substantial public investment into the green transition through institutions like the *KfW Bankengruppe*,

rather than relying extensively on public bond markets. France's dirigiste tradition similarly emphasises strategic state involvement.

Japan's historically bank-centric financial system also aligns with this model. Although their public "green debt" issuance may be less prominent, these countries pursue robust greening through regulatory frameworks and targeted lending. Their financial-sector emissions profiles and policy structures reflect a state-supervised approach, distinct from the market-driven strategies of Cluster 1.

While the statistical basis for this bifurcation is limited, the theoretical coherence is compelling. The findings highlight that the financial pillar of the Post-Schumpeterian transition is not homogeneous; it aligns closely with each country's institutional configuration. The G-7 exemplifies how even among advanced economies, green finance strategies diverge along traditional lines between Anglo-Saxon market systems and the state-led, bank-centric models of Continental Europe and Japan.

3.7.3 Green Finance in the BRICS Countries

The G-19 analysis underscores that BRICS nations are developing green finance frameworks in diverse, nationally specific ways. Unlike the G-7, the BRICS do not fit a simple dichotomy between market-led and state-influenced models. The cluster analysis (see Fig. 3.7) places them across different groups, reflecting varied institutional structures and policy priorities.

China and Russia are included in Cluster 1, which denotes countries with expanding, state-driven green finance initiatives. These efforts are largely shaped by government policy and public financial institutions, even though green debt markets remain less developed.

India and South Africa appear in Cluster 2, characterised by dynamic green financial sectors. Their alignment with market-led economies like the United States and the United Kingdom suggests greater reliance on capital markets and the issuance of green bonds, potentially reflecting historical linkages to market-oriented financial systems.

Brazil falls into Cluster 3, alongside technologically advanced economies exhibiting uneven progress. Its financial sector does not conform strictly to either the state-led or market-led archetype. Brazil's intermediate position indicates a system still in the process of defining its strategy for mobilising green finance.

This variation within the BRICS underscores that their financial strategies for the green transition are adapting to local institutional conditions. Rather than converging on a unified model, each country is navigating the transition within the constraints and opportunities of its own political economy. As with the G-7, the Post-Schumpeterian transformation in the BRICS context reflects institutional diversity rather than convergence.

3.8 Comprehensive Analysis of Post-Schumpetarian Green Transformation

In the final empirical section, we broaden our analysis of green technology and green patents by incorporating national GDP and greenhouse gas emissions. This expanded perspective provides an initial indication of the extent to which the NIS of the G-19 countries integrate both existing and future-oriented climate mitigation technologies with observable economic growth and associated CO_2 emissions. The aim is to develop a holistic understanding of the transformation processes within the G-19, including both the G-7 and BRICS nations, capturing present dynamics and potential future trajectories.

We begin with a cluster analysis of the G-19 countries, which offers a preliminary overview of the Post-Schumpeterian status of each member's economic system relative to the group as a whole.

3.8.1 G-19 Countries

Figure 3.8 presents a cluster analysis of the G-19 economies, using key indicators related to PSE. These indicators include GDP growth rate, EV sales, total greenhouse gas emissions, CO_2 emissions per unit of GDP (measured in purchasing power parity, PPP), and the number of Y02 patents. The optimal number of clusters, determined via the Duda–Hart pseudo T-squared statistic, is four. Each cluster is characterised as follows:

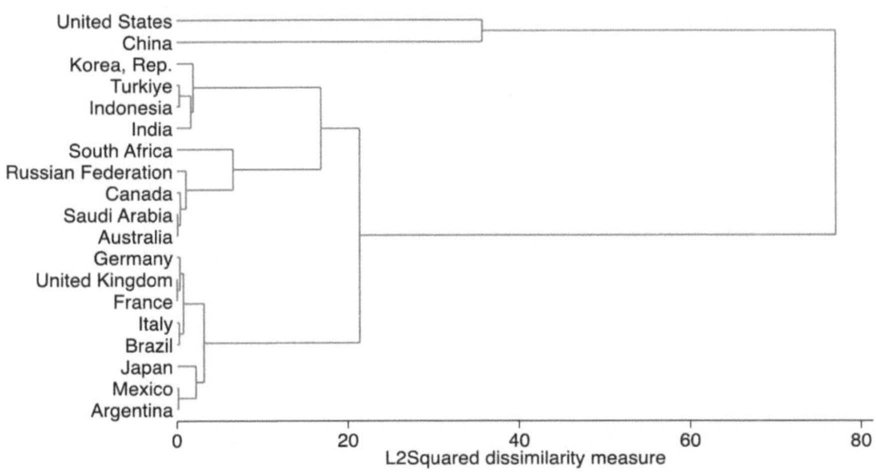

Fig. 3.8 Cluster analysis for greening economic systems

Cluster 1: High-Stakes Innovators (United States and China)
This cluster consists of the United States and China, two of the world's largest economies. Despite differing political and economic systems, both countries share key features in their green innovation profiles. Each demonstrates robust GDP growth, with China showing more rapid expansion in recent decades. Both are global leaders in EV sales, supported by market scale and policy incentives. These nations are also among the highest contributors to global greenhouse gas emissions, driven by their industrial structures and large populations. However, their significant investments in green technology, as reflected in high Y02 patent counts, suggest active engagement in climate mitigation through technological innovation. They are simultaneously major emitters and frontrunners in the development of solutions.

Cluster 2: Advanced and Balanced Transformers (Germany, United Kingdom, France, Italy, Australia and Japan)
This group includes high-income economies characterised by strong green innovation capacity, particularly in Y02 patent activity. Japan, historically a pioneer in environmental technology, especially in energy efficiency, automotive innovation, and clean energy, illustrates this trend. These countries tend to report lower greenhouse gas emissions per unit of GDP, indicating a degree of decoupling between economic growth and emissions. High EV adoption rates, particularly in Europe and Japan, reflect the impact of stringent environmental regulations and strong domestic industrial capabilities. While GDP growth in this group is more moderate than in Cluster 1, these economies maintain a stable trajectory that balances economic development with environmental goals.

Cluster 3: Emerging and Advancing Economies (South Korea, Turkey, Indonesia, India, South Africa, Brazil, Mexico, and Argentina)
This cluster comprises emerging and middle-income economies, many of which exhibit moderate to high GDP growth driven by industrialisation and expanding consumer markets. However, their levels of green technological innovation, as indicated by Y02 patent activity, remain relatively modest. EV adoption is in the early stages, although it is expected to increase as these countries invest further in sustainable transport. Greenhouse gas emissions vary within this cluster, reflecting diverse development paths and energy usage. Nonetheless, a growing interest in green technologies suggests future potential for innovation-led sustainability.

Cluster 4: Resource-Dependent Economies (Russian Federation, Canada, and Saudi Arabia)
The final cluster includes economies heavily reliant on natural resource extraction, particularly fossil fuels. Consequently, they exhibit high greenhouse gas emissions per unit of GDP, reflecting the carbon-intensive nature of their economic structures. Although these countries have made some progress in green innovation, as evidenced by moderate Y02 patent activity, they lag behind the other clusters. EV sales are low, likely due to weaker policy incentives and lower urgency for energy

transition. Nevertheless, increasing global demand for clean energy may prompt strategic shifts in these economies.

In summary, the analysis reveals substantial divergence among G-19 countries in terms of integrating economic growth with climate mitigation strategies. The United States and China lead in green innovation despite high emissions; emerging economies are in the early stages of transition; and resource-dependent economies face more structural challenges but retain potential for future transformation. This cluster-based analysis offers insight into the varied pathways nations are pursuing in their movement towards sustainable economic systems.

3.8.2 G-7's Divergent Paths

To examine the green transition within the G-7, we conducted a dedicated cluster analysis. The Duda–Hart test indicated two optimal clusters, revealing a pronounced divergence in green transformation strategies among these advanced economies. This bifurcation illustrates distinct Post-Schumpeterian archetypes emerging within the G-7.

Cluster 1: The United States as the 'High-Stakes Innovator'
The United States forms a standalone cluster, underscoring its distinctive profile. It combines high GDP growth with world-leading green patent output (Y02) and very high total greenhouse gas emissions. This configuration typifies a high-risk, high-reward Schumpeterian model: the United States is both a major contributor to climate change and a principal driver of technological solutions.

This approach aligns with the concept of a 'Supervised Positive Sum Policy' introduced in the theoretical section of this study. Ambitious industrial policies such as the Inflation Reduction Act (IRA) exemplify this model, which emphasises large-scale public and private investment over regulatory constraints or carbon pricing. It represents a strategy of transformative innovation at scale, tolerating current emissions in the pursuit of disruptive green technologies.

Cluster 2: The 'Consensus and Convergence' Group

This cluster comprises the remaining six G-7 nations, reflecting a more incremental and coordinated path towards green transformation. While these countries also lead in green innovation, particularly Germany and Japan, their strategic emphasis differs from that of the United States.

Their approach combines green technology development with broader climate policy frameworks. Regulatory standards and market mechanisms, such as the EU Emissions Trading System, play a significant role, especially in France, Germany, Italy, and the United Kingdom. These nations generally exhibit more moderate GDP growth. Their decarbonisation strategies focus on emission reduction through regulatory compliance, industrial adaptation, and efficiency improvements.

Japan exemplifies a long-standing commitment to energy efficiency and technological refinement, whereas Canada's profile is influenced by its resource-based economy. For the European members, the European Green Deal provides a unifying regulatory framework for their transition strategies.

The division of the G-7 into two distinct clusters is one of the most salient findings of this analysis. It demonstrates that no singular pathway defines green transformation among advanced economies. Instead, at least two models are emerging: an innovation-led, high-growth American model, and a pan-industrial, regulatory-guided approach focused on steady transition. This divergence has significant implications for geo-economic competition and the future of global leadership in green technology.

3.8.3 Profiles of the BRICS Countries

The comprehensive analysis confirms the significant heterogeneity within the BRICS group. The G-19 cluster analysis presented in Fig. 3.8 dispersed the BRICS nations across three of the four identified archetypes, illustrating that they are pursuing fundamentally different transformation pathways.

China's profile is particularly noteworthy. It was grouped with the United States in the first cluster, identified as the 'high-stakes innovators'. This categorisation reflects China's distinctive combination of sustained GDP growth, world-leading green patent activity, a vast EV market, and concurrently, some of the highest greenhouse gas emissions globally. China thus occupies a central and paradoxical position in the global transformation, serving both as a principal source of emissions and as a key driver of technological solutions.

India, Brazil, and South Africa were classified within the third cluster of 'emerging and advancing economies'. Although each country faces unique national conditions, they share the common challenge of balancing economic development and industrialisation with the imperative of emissions reduction. Their NISs remain in developmental stages, and their adoption of green technologies is less advanced than that of the leading economies, placing them on a slower and more incremental transformation trajectory.

The Russian Federation, in contrast, was assigned to the fourth cluster of 'resource-dependent economies'. Its economic model, heavily reliant on fossil fuel exports, exerts a defining influence on its transformation profile. This structural dependency constrains green innovation and the uptake of clean technologies, thereby hindering progress towards a Post-Schumpeterian transition.

In summary, the analysis reinforces the conclusion that, while BRICS remains a significant geopolitical and economic grouping, it does not represent a coherent bloc in the context of green transformation. The group comprises a global innovation leader (China), large emerging economies navigating the complex interplay between growth and sustainability (India, Brazil, South Africa), and a resource-dependent state facing deep structural barriers (Russia). These divergent profiles underscore the necessity of country-specific, rather than bloc-based, strategies in the formulation of effective global climate policies.

3.9 Summary of the Empirical Study

The empirical section investigates the transition of G-20 countries, particularly the G-7 and BRICS, towards a green transformation. Employing a systematic analytical framework and statistical methods, the study examines the relationships among economic growth, emissions, innovation, and finance. The dataset comprises national-level indicators, with variable significance assessed using the Friedman non-parametric test to eliminate redundancy. Cluster analysis, based on the Ward method and supported by the elbow and Duda–Hart tests, identifies groups of countries exhibiting structural similarities and divergences in their transition pathways.

The first empirical theme concerns the long-debated issue of decoupling, defined as the severance of the traditional link between economic growth and environmental degradation. Absolute decoupling, whereby economies grow while emissions decline in absolute terms, is presented as the ultimate sustainability benchmark. An analysis of G-19 countries using GDP growth and CO_2 emissions per unit of GDP yields three broad clusters. The first includes the United States, China, India, South Korea, Turkey, and Indonesia, economies experiencing high growth alongside substantial emissions intensity, reflecting either reindustrialisation or catch-up industrialisation. The second cluster (Russia, Saudi Arabia, South Africa, and Canada) comprises resource-dependent economies with moderate growth and a strong reliance on fossil fuels. The third cluster, comprising the United Kingdom, France, Germany, and Japan, represents advanced industrialised economies characterised by lower emissions per unit of GDP and relative decoupling, albeit coupled with slower overall growth.

Within the G-7, the variation is even more pronounced. The United States and Canada exemplify a resource-intensive, innovation-led model marked by slower decoupling. The United Kingdom and France have achieved post-industrial decoupling, facilitated by regulation and nuclear energy. Italy occupies a transitional position due to structural weaknesses, while Germany and Japan, as industrial powerhouses, pursue state-supervised green transformations constrained by the legacy of carbon-intensive sectors. Among the BRICS, each member follows a distinct trajectory. China and India are large-scale emitters with starkly different levels of total factor productivity. Russia and South Africa are carbon-intensive resource economies, whereas Brazil, though comparable to Germany in total emissions, differs markedly in sectoral structure. These findings demonstrate that bloc classifications obscure underlying structural diversity.

The study next examines NISs through the dual lens of applied green technologies and forward-looking green patents. For applied technologies, indicators include renewable energy generation and capacity, alongside EV sales. Four clusters emerge. The first, comprising Canada, Brazil, Saudi Arabia, and China, shows either a strong renewable energy baseline or rapid EV growth, though not both. The second (Russia, Indonesia, South Africa, and South Korea) remains heavily fossil-fuel dependent, with gradual transitions. The third cluster, comprising the United Kingdom, Turkey, Italy, Germany, the United States, and France, demonstrates consistent progress in both renewables and EVs. The fourth cluster (Argentina, India, Japan, Mexico, and Australia) continues to rely heavily on fossil fuels, with underdeveloped EV markets.

Within the G-7, two strategic orientations are discernible. A policy-balanced group (Canada, Germany, Italy, and the United Kingdom) advances in both renewables and EVs. In contrast, France, Japan, and the United States pursue more specialised strategies based on nuclear power, technological expertise, or market scale. Among the BRICS, adoption patterns are fragmented. China is a paradoxical leader in EV deployment yet relies heavily on coal. Brazil combines clean electricity with weak transport electrification. Russia and South Africa remain slow adopters, constrained by fossil-fuel dependence, while India's transition is early-stage and hampered by scale limitations.

Forward-oriented innovation is assessed through green patent activity, classified under Y02 and Y04S categories. Four clusters are identified. The United States, Japan, South Korea, and China constitute global leaders, exhibiting broad and intensive patenting across multiple green technology domains. Germany, the United Kingdom, and France form a significant European group, with specialisations in adaptation technologies, energy-efficient buildings, and smart grids. A third group (Italy, India, Australia, and Canada) shows moderate and diverse but less prominent innovation. The final group (Russia, Brazil, Mexico, Turkey, South Africa, Saudi Arabia, Indonesia, and Argentina) registers low levels of green patenting, indicating a dependence on technology transfer from more advanced economies. Within the G-7, a three-tier structure is evident: the United States and Japan at the frontier; Germany, the United Kingdom, and France as specialised core contributors; and Italy and Canada as steady but less dominant participants. Among BRICS, only China aligns with the global frontier; India emerges as a rising moderate innovator, while Brazil, Russia, and South Africa lag behind, highlighting the necessity of imported expertise to advance.

The financial sector is assessed through three indicators: climate-related financial policy frameworks (CRFPI), green bond issuance, and the carbon intensity of bank lending. Four clusters emerge. China, Russia, Saudi Arabia, and Mexico are expanding green financial initiatives, though at different rates. The United States, United Kingdom, India, and South Africa lead with dynamic, market-driven green finance, underpinned by active bond markets. Indonesia, South Korea, Japan, and Brazil form a middle group of technologically advanced economies with uneven progress in financial decarbonisation. Canada, Turkey, and Argentina fall behind in adopting green financial policies and instruments.

Within the G-7, although no sharp statistical divisions arise, a subtle bifurcation is evident. Canada, Italy, the United Kingdom, and the United States embody the Anglo-Saxon model, characterised by deep capital markets and market-led green debt issuance. France, Germany, and Japan, by contrast, reflect more state-influenced, bank-centric systems in which public development banks and regulatory oversight play greater roles. The BRICS exhibit similarly varied approaches. China and Russia focus on state-led expansion; India and South Africa emphasise market-based instruments; and Brazil occupies a mixed position, reflecting both models.

Overall, financial strategies reflect each country's institutional configuration rather than convergence on a unified model.

Finally, the study synthesises indicators of GDP growth, EV sales, total greenhouse gas emissions, CO_2 intensity, and green patenting to construct a comprehensive profile of 'greening economic systems'. Four G-19 clusters are identified. The United States and China form one group, characterised by high growth, significant innovation, and very high emissions. Germany, the United Kingdom, France, Italy, Australia, and Japan constitute a second cluster of advanced economies with lower emissions intensity, robust patenting, and strong EV adoption, albeit with more moderate growth. The third group (South Korea, Turkey, Indonesia, India, South Africa, Brazil, Mexico, and Argentina) includes emerging economies that are progressing in green innovation and adoption but remain limited in scale. The final cluster (Russia, Canada, and Saudi Arabia) comprises resource-dependent economies with high emissions and weak green technology uptake.

Within the G-7, a stark division is apparent. The United States stands alone as a 'high-stakes innovator', combining strong growth and patent leadership with the highest emissions. The remaining six G-7 members follow a more convergent, regulation-led transition characterised by moderate growth and consistent innovation.

Three key conclusions emerge across all analytical dimensions. First, G-7 and BRICS affiliations are poor predictors of green transition pathways; structural conditions, resource endowments, and institutional frameworks exert far greater influence than geopolitical labels. Second, distinct Post-Schumpeterian archetypes are taking shape: a high-stakes, innovation-led disruption model (exemplified by the United States and China in its state-led variant); a balanced, policy-driven decarbonisation model (as seen in core Europe and Japan); and a range of catch-up strategies among emerging economies that must balance growth, affordability, and capacity building. Third, the momentum of green transformation hinges on the co-evolution of three pillars: technology (both current and prospective), markets, and finance. Countries that align innovation frontiers, scalable deployment (e.g., renewables and EVs), and effective financial architectures are best positioned to translate green innovation into competitive advantage and sustained decoupling.

In conclusion, the empirical findings support the thesis presented in Chap. 2: the green transition will be plural, path-dependent, and supervision-intensive. NISs and the financial pillar will jointly determine whether economies can successfully undertake a Post-Schumpeterian, positive-sum shift from brown to green.

3.10 Concluding Remarks

This study concludes with reflections on the current global context in which political measures aimed at addressing climate change intersect with the pursuit of economic growth. Achieving global emission reductions and temperature targets requires coordinated efforts by all countries, advanced, emerging, and developing alike. Each must adapt to climate change, mitigate its adverse effects, and transition from 'brown' to 'green' modes of economic activity. Climate change is not a national problem; it is a global challenge that demands collective commitment and cooperation from the international community. With this in mind, it is pertinent to briefly consider the geo-economic context of the global 'quest for transformation' as it has unfolded over recent decades.

Empirical findings suggest a striking conclusion: in the global green transformation, the United States and China occupy a distinctive and dominant position that is reshaping both the geo-economic and geopolitical order. These two countries differ markedly from other G-19 members, not only due to their economic scale but also because they simultaneously represent the world's largest emitters and its most dynamic centres of green innovation. They thus embody a paradox: while both are primary contributors to climate change, they are also among the most significant sources of technological solutions. This dual role renders them indispensable actors in the transition towards a Post-Schumpeterian world economy.

From a geo-economic standpoint, the United States and China constitute a de facto technological duopoly. They lead in applied green technologies, such as EVs and renewable energy systems, and dominate innovation in climate mitigation technologies, as evidenced by patent activity across multiple sectors. While other major economies, particularly the European Union and Japan, retain strength in specific niches, they are increasingly confined to specialised technological domains. The frontier of industrial value creation in batteries, hydrogen, smart grids, and advanced clean energy is now being shaped more in Washington and Beijing than in Berlin, Paris, or Tokyo.

Nonetheless, the two leaders pursue divergent models of transformation. The United States combines market dynamism with state-guided industrial policy. The Inflation Reduction Act exemplifies this approach by deploying large-scale subsidies and incentives to mobilise private investment and innovation, while preserving the predominantly market-driven structure of the economy. By contrast, China directs its transition through centralised state leadership, long-term industrial strategies, and substantial investment in production scaling, often implemented by private firms. While both models aim to accelerate green industrial development, they reflect distinct institutional logics. The United States positions government as a supportive facilitator, whereas China relies on private enterprise to introduce flexibility within a state-coordinated framework. This asymmetry intensifies the systemic rivalry between the two, rendering the green transformation not merely an economic process but also a contest between alternative capitalist models.

Geopolitically, both countries employ their technological capabilities as tools of strategic influence. The United States seeks to secure alliances around key supply chains (batteries, semiconductors, and critical raw materials) through 'friendshoring' and targeted trade agreements. China, for its part, exports green infrastructure and technologies via the Belt and Road Initiative, integrating emerging economies into its industrial ecosystem. As a result, decarbonisation has become a domain of strategic competition, where technological advancement serves both economic and diplomatic purposes.

Simultaneously, this rivalry contributes to a fragmented international landscape. Analyses of the BRICS and G-7 reveal that countries follow divergent transformation trajectories, shaped more by domestic structures and resource endowments than by geopolitical alignments. Emerging and resource-dependent economies face difficult choices: whether to align with US- or China-led technological platforms, to pursue independent specialisations, or to risk increasing dependency. Rather than convergence on a single developmental pathway, the global order is likely to remain characterised by varied national strategies orbiting the US-China duopoly.

Despite this competition, the interdependence between the United States and China remains critical. Both contribute disproportionately to global emissions, and both are essential to scaling green technologies. Their rivalry could drive technological progress, generating positive spillovers for other economies (Feng et al., 2025). However, it also risks provoking geopolitical tensions, including protectionist policies, green trade conflicts, and barriers to international cooperation. The key challenge lies in managing this rivalry to foster innovation and diffusion without further fragmenting the global response to climate change.

In summary, the United States and China have emerged as the central poles of the Post-Schumpeterian transformation. They are at once competitors and co-producers of the global energy transition, influencing the future green economy through their domestic policy choices and their impact on international markets, supply chains, and governance frameworks. For other major actors (Europe, Japan, India, Brazil, and beyond), this new configuration requires adaptation to a world in which green leadership is increasingly concentrated in two rival centres of power. Just as oil defined geopolitical influence in the twentieth century, and digital technologies did in the early twenty-first, the competition for green technology leadership is becoming the core of twenty-first-century geo-economic rivalry (The Economist, 2020). The success of the global transformation will depend not only on technological progress but also on the evolving balance between competition and cooperation between Washington and Beijing.

Appendix

Table A.1 Indicator List for Clustering Analysis

Indicators	Data Source	Data Length
RE share of electricity generation (%)	Internnational Renewable Energy Agency (IRENA)	2000–2022
RE share of electricity capacity (%)	Internnational Renewable Energy Agency (IRENA)	2000–2023
EV Car Sales	Internationl Energey Agency (IEA)	2010–2023
Y02 Patents	Patents View (USPTO)	2010–2023
CO2 emissions per purchasing power parity (PPP) of GDP	World Bank Open Data/Climate Watch. 2020. GHG Emissions. Washington, DC: World Resources Institute. Available at: climatewatchdata.org/ghg-emissions.	1990–2020
Total greenhouse gas emissions (kt of CO2 equivalent)	World Bank Open Data/Climate Watch Historical GHG Emissions (1990–2020). 2023. Washington, DC: World Resources Institute.	1990–2020
GDP Growth Rate	World Bank Open Data/World Bank national accounts data, and OECD National Accounts data files.	1961–2023
Climate related Financial Policy Index (CRFPI)	Dataset for the climate-related financial policy index (CRFPI), https://zenodo.org/records/7599914	2010–2023
Green Debt	https://climatedata.imf.org/pages/climate-finance#cf2	2010–2023
Carbon Footprint of Bank Loans	https://climatedata.imf.org/pages/climate-finance#cf1	2010–2023

H. Hanusch, Y. Hara, *Innovative Growth and Climate Security*, SpringerBriefs in Economics, https://doi.org/10.1007/978-981-92-1005-3

References

Andreessen, M. (2023). The technooptimist manifesto. *a16z*. https://a16z.com/the-techno-optimist-manifesto/

Bearak, M. (2023, September 6). At Africa's first climate summit, a clear call to the world: invest in us. *The New York Times*. https://www.nytimes.com/2023/09/06/world/africa/africa-climate-summit-nairobi-declaration.html

Beck, U. (1986). *Risikogesellschaft: Auf dem Weg in eine andere Moderne*. Suhrkamp Verlag.

Beckert, J. (2024). *Verkaufte Zukunft*. Suhrkamp Verlag.

Boulding, K. E. (1962). Notes on a theory of philanthropy. In F. G. Dickinson (Ed.), *Philanthropy and public policy* (pp. 57–72). National Bureau of Economic Research.

Brett, C. (2024). *The price is wrong: Why capitalism won't save the planet*. Biteback Publishing.

Brynjolfsson, E. (1993). The productivity paradox of informationtechnology. *Communications of the Association for Computing Machinery, 36*(12), 66–77. https://doi.org/10.1145/163298.163309

Bundesregierung Deutschland. (2019). Gesetz zur Einführung eines BundesKlimaschutzgesetzes und zur Änderung weiterer Vorschriften. Bundesgesetzblatt Jahrgang 2019 Teil I Nr. 51. https://www.bgbl.de/xaver/bgbl/start.xav%3Fstartbk%3DBundesanzeiger_BGBl%26jumpTo%3Dbgbl119s2513.pdf

CDP. (2023). Disclosure data factsheet 2023. https://www.cdp.net/en/insights/cdp-2023-disclosure-data-factsheet

Christian, D. (2018). *Origin story: A big history of everything*. Little, Brown and Company.

Christian, D., Brown, C. S., & Benjamin, C. (2013). *Big history: Between nothing and everything*. McGrawHill Professional.

Clark, M. A., Springmann, M., Rayner, M., & Scarborough, P. (2022). Estimating the environmental impacts of 57,000 food products. *Proceedings of the National Academy of Sciences, 119*(33), e2120584119. https://doi.org/10.1073/pnas.2120584119

Coy, P. (2023, September 13). An economic case against environmental doomsayers. *The New York Times*. https://www.nytimes.com/2023/09/13/opinion/climate-change-doomsayers-economy.html

Cullenward, D., & Victor, D. G. (2020). *Making climate policy work*. Polity Press.

de Freitas, V., Netto, S., Sobral, M. F. F., Ribeiro, A. R. B., & Soares, G. R. D. L. (2020). Concepts and forms of greenwashing: A systematic review. *Environmental Sciences Europe, 32*(1)., Article 19. https://doi.org/10.1186/s12302-020-0300-3

Douglas, B. D., & Brauer, M. (2021). Gamification to prevent climate change: A review of games and apps for sustainability. *Current Opinion in Psychology, 42*, 89–94. https://doi.org/10.1016/j.copsyc.2021.05.005

H. Hanusch, Y. Hara, *Innovative Growth and Climate Security*, SpringerBriefs in Economics, https://doi.org/10.1007/978-981-92-1005-3

Douthat, R. (2025, June 25). Peter Thiel and the Antichrist. The original tech right power player on AI, Mars and immortality. In: *Interesting Times, The New York Times*. https://www.nytimes.com/2025/06/26/opinion/peter-thiel-antichrist-ross-douthat.html
Fagerberg, J. (2003). Schumpeter and the revival of evolutionary economics: An appraisal of the literature. *Journal of Evolutionary Economics, 13*(2), 125–159. https://doi.org/10.1007/s00191-003-0144-1
Feenstra, R. C., Inklaar, R., & Timmer, M. P. (2015). The Next Generation of the Penn World Table. *American Economic Review, 105*(10), 3150–3182.
Feng, A., Li, H., & Wang, Y. (2025). We are all in the same boat: Cross border spillovers of climate risk through international trade and supply chain. *The Economic Journal, 135*, 1433–1466.
Friedman, M. (1937). The use of ranks to avoid the assumption of normality implicit in the analysis of variance. *Journal of the American Statistical Association, 32*(200), 675–701.
GeorgescuRoegen, N. (1971). *The entropy law and the economic process*. Harvard University Press.
Gordon, R. J. (2016). *The rise and fall of American growth: The U.S. standard of living since the Civil War*. Princeton University Press.
Haberl, H., et al. (2020). A systematic review of the evidence for decoupling of greenhouse gas emissions from economic growth. *Environmental Research Letters, 15*(6), 063001.
Hall, B. H. (Ed.). (2013). *Handbook of the economics of innovation*. North Holland.
Hanusch, H. (1972). *Theorie des öffentlichen Gutes: Allokative und distributive Aspekte*. Vandenhoeck & Ruprecht.
Hanusch, H. (2011). *NutzenKostenAnalyse* (3rd ed.). Vahlen.
Hanusch, H., & Pyka, A. (2007a). The principles of NeoSchumpeterian economics. *Cambridge Journal of Economics, 31*(2), 275–289. https://doi.org/10.1093/cje/bel018
Hanusch, H., & Pyka, A. (Eds.). (2007b). *Elgar companion to NeoSchumpeterian economics*. Edward Elgar Publishing.
Harari, Y. N. (2017a). *Homo Deus: A brief history of tomorrow*. Harper.
Harari, Y. N. (2017b). Reboot for the AI revolution. *Nature, 550*, 324–327. https://doi.org/10.1038/550324a
Härdle, W., & Simar, L. (2007). *Applied multivariate statistical analysis*. Springer.
Hayek, F. A. (1944). *The road to serfdom*. University of Chicago Press.
Hayek, F. A. (1969). Der Wettbewerb als Entdeckungsverfahren. In *Freiburger Studien* (pp. 249–265). J. C. B. Mohr (Paul Siebeck).
Intergovernmental Panel on Climate Change. (2023). *Climate change 2023: Synthesis report. Contribution of Working Groups I, II and III to the Sixth Assessment Report of the Intergovernmental Panel on Climate Change*. IPCC. https://www.ipcc.ch/report/ar6/syr/
Jobson, J. D. (1992). Principal components, factors and correspondence analysis. In *Applied multivariate data analysis. Springer texts in statistics*. Springer.
Jones, C. I. (2002). *Introduction to economic growth*. W. W. Norton & Company.
Kahneman, D., Lovallo, D., & Sibony, O. (2019, May 21). A structured approach to strategic decisions. *MIT Sloan Management Review*. https://sloanreview.mit.edu/article/a-structured-approach-to-strategic-decisions/
Kallis, G. (2011). In defense of degrowth. *Ecological Economics, 70*(5), 873–880. https://doi.org/10.1016/j.ecolecon.2010.12.007
Leibenstein, H. (1966). Allocative efficiency vs. "Xefficiency". *American Economic Review, 56*(3), 392–415.
Lundvall, B.-Å. (2005). National Innovation Systems, Analytical Concept and development tool. Paper presented at the DRUID conference Copenhagen, June 27–29, 2005.
Lundvall, B.-Å. (Ed.). (2010). *National systems of innovation: Towards a theory of innovation and interactive learning*. Anthem Press.
Mathiesen, K. (2022, November 6). Populists vs. the planet: How climate became the new culture war front line. *Politico*. https://www.politico.eu/article/populists-vs-the-planet-how-climate-became-the-new-culture-war-front-line/

Mazzucato, M. (2013). *The entrepreneurial state: Debunking public versus private sector myths.* Anthem Press.

Mazzucato, M., Songwe, V., Assunção, J., Buchner, B., Gabor, D., Kohli, R., Lebdioui, A., Lopes, C., Ma, J., Palacios, L., & Volz, U. (2024). *A green and just planet: The 1.5 °C agenda for governing global industrial and financial policies in the G20.* Independent Report of the G20 TFCLIMA Group of Experts.

McAfee, A. (2019). *More from less: The surprising story of how we learned to prosper using fewer resources—and what happens next.* Scribner.

Meadows, D. H., Meadows, D. L., Randers, J., & Behrens, W. W., III. (1972). *The limits to growth.* Universe Books.

Nelson, R. R. (Ed.). (1993). *National innovation systems: A comparative analysis.* Oxford University Press.

Network for Greening the Financial System. (2019). A call for action: Climate change as a source of financial risk. https://www.ngfs.net/sites/default/files/medias/documents/ngfs_first_comprehensive_report_-_17042019_0.pdf

Nordhaus, W. D. (1992). *The "DICE" model: Background and structure of a dynamic interfaced climateeconomy model of the economics of global warming* (Cowles Foundation Discussion Paper No. 1009). Yale University.

Ord, T. (2020). *The precipice: Existential risk and the future of humanity.* Hachette Books.

Ostrom, E., Dietz, T., Dolsak, N., Stern, P. C., Stonich, S., & Weber, E. U. (Eds.). (2002). *The drama of the commons.* National Academy Press.

Polanyi, K. (1944). *The great transformation: The political and economic origins of our time.* Farrar & Rinehart.

Pope Francis. (2015). *Laudato si': On care for our common home [Encyclical letter].* Vatican Press. https://www.vatican.va/content/francesco/en/encyclicals/documents/papa-francesco_20150524_enciclica-laudato-si.html

Postman, N. (1993). *Technopoly: The surrender of culture to technology.* Vintage Books.

Rifkin, J. (2022). *The age of resilience: Reimagining existence on a rewilding earth.* St. Martin's Press.

Romer, P. M. (1990). Endogenous technological change. *Journal of Political Economy, 98*(5, Pt. 2), S71–S102. https://doi.org/10.1086/261725

Rushkoff, D. (2023). *Survival of the richest: Escape fantasies of the tech billionaires.* W. W. Norton & Company.

Saito, K. (2023). *Marx in the Anthropocene: Towards the idea of degrowth communism.* Cambridge University Press.

Sarkodie, S. A., Adams, S., & Leirvik, T. (2023). Comprehensive green growth indicators across countries and territories. *Scientific Data, 10*, Article 413. https://doi.org/10.1038/s41597-023-02324-7

Saviotti, P. P., & Pyka, A. (2004). Economic development by the creation of new sectors. *Journal of Evolutionary Economics, 14*, 1–35. https://doi.org/10.1007/s00191-004-0183-2

Schmitt, C. (1996). *The concept of the political.* University of Chicago Press. (Original work published 1932).

Schumpeter, J. A. (1934). *The theory of economic development: An inquiry into profits, capital, credit, interest, and the business cycle.* Harvard University Press. (Original work published 1911).

Schumpeter, J. A. (1942). *Capitalism, socialism and democracy.* Harper & Brothers.

Siemens. (2022). *Sustainability report 2022: Strong performance and accelerated progress.* Siemens AG.

Slobodian, Q. (2025). *Hayek's Bastards: Race, Gold, IQ, and the Capitalism of the Far Right.* Zone Books.

Slobodian, Q., & Tarnoff, B. (2026). *Muskism. A guide for the perplexed.* Harper.

Stern, N. H. (2007). *The economics of climate change: The Stern review.* Cambridge University Press.

Stiglitz, J. E., Sen, A., & Fitoussi, J.-P. (2009). *Report by the commission on the measurement of economic performance and social progress*. Commission on the Measurement of Economic Performance and Social Progress.

Suleiman, M., & Bhaskar, M. (2023). *The coming wave: Technology, power, and the 21st century's greatest dilemma*. Crown.

Susskind, D. (2024). *Growth: A reckoning*. Allen Lane.

The Economist. (2020, September 19). *Power in the 21st century [Special Report]*. The Economist.

The Economist. (2023, September 16). *How AI can revolutionize science*. The Economist.

True cost accounting of food. (2021). True cost accounting of food. *Nature Food, 2*, 629. https://doi.org/10.1038/s43016-021-00379-6

Tuccille, J. (1970). *Radical libertarianism: A right wing alternative*. Bobbs Merrill.

Tupy, M. L., & Pooley, G. L. (2023). *Superabundance: The story of population growth, innovation, and human flourishing on an infinitely bountiful planet*. Cato Institute.

U.S. Government. (2022). Inflation Reduction Act of 2022, Pub. L. No. 117169, 136 Stat. 1818. https://www.congress.gov/bill/117th-congress/house-bill/5376

United Nations. (2023). *The sustainable development goals report: Special edition*. https://unstats.un.org/sdgs/report/2023/The-Sustainable-Development-Goals-Report-2023_Special-Edition.pdf

USAID (U.S. Agency for International Development). (2024). *FY 2025 annual performance report*. https://www.state.gov/wp-content/uploads/2025/02/FY_2024-APR_01-17-2024_Compliant-PDF.pdf

Wagner, G. (2021). *Geoengineering: The gamble*. Polity Press.

Wang, D. (2025). *Breakneck: China's quest to engineer the future*. Allen Lane.

World Economic Forum. (2023). *Global risks report 2023*. https://www.weforum.org/publications/global-risks-report-2023/

Index

H. Hanusch, Y. Hara, *Innovative Growth and Climate Security*, SpringerBriefs in Economics, https://doi.org/10.1007/978-981-92-1005-3

MIX
Papier aus verantwortungsvollen Quellen
Paper from responsible sources
FSC® C105338

If you have any concerns about our products,
you can contact us on
ProductSafety@springernature.com

In case Publisher is established outside the EU,
the EU authorized representative is:
Springer Nature Customer Service Center GmbH
Europaplatz 3, 69115 Heidelberg, Germany

Printed by Libri Plureos GmbH
in Hamburg, Germany